ANGELS WITH

love
Ishmael
xx

By the same author:
    The History of Ishmael Part 1

Angels with Dirty Faces

ISHMAEL

KINGSWAY PUBLICATIONS
EASTBOURNE

Biblical quotations are from the
New International Version © International Bible Society
1973, 1978, 1984. Published by Hodder & Stoughton.

Front cover design by John Herbert

British Library Cataloguing in Publication Data

Ishmael
    Angels with dirty faces.
    1. Christian church. Role of children
    I. Title
    262'.15

    ISBN 0-86065-717-5

Production and printing in Great Britain for
KINGSWAY PUBLICATIONS LTD
Lottbridge Drove, Eastbourne, E. Sussex BN23 6NT by
Nuprint Ltd, 30b Station Road, Harpenden, Herts AL5 4SE.

I dedicate this book to all those faithful parents and children's workers who have done their jobs well yet may have received little or no credit for it.

Contents

Acknowledgements

Many thanks to my wife Irene, and to my children, Joseph, Daniel and Suzy—my favourite little angels—whose help, and encouragement have been invaluable to me while I have beeen working on this book.

Thanks also to my Glorie Company Band and team of workers—where would I be without them?—and all my 'adopted' children worldwide who have taught me so much.

Thanks to all those who have helped me get my thoughts on paper, namely, Irene, David Thatcher, Clive Price and Mike Morris. Thanks to Lynton Hemsley for his artwork, David for the photography, Irene for the cover idea and design, and the little chap on the back cover whose photo was sent to me—I still don't know his name.

Finally a special dedication to my little nephew Benjamin who I know is one day looking forward to working with his Uncle Ishmael. Benjamin, I'll try and stay young, just for you.

Ishmael is available both nationally and internationally to come and lead seminars in more detail on the subjects mentioned in this book. He can be contacted by writing to: PO Box 828, Rustington, Littlehampton, West Sussex BN16 3NS, England.

For details of Ishmael's Glorie products, please enclose a stamped addressed envelope.

Introduction

Dad has asked us three to write the introduction to his book, so here we go!

My first recollection of my dad is when I was about nine months old and he accidentally tipped my pram up and I fell face first onto the pavement. I miraculously escaped without a scratch, but Dad has never been the same since.

I can remember when I was about two years old, at teatimes I would sometimes fall asleep while eating my tea and Dad used to lift me out of my high chair and make me run around the garden to wake me up so that I could finish my tea.

As I got older I remember being proud of my dad as I appeared on stage with him and the rest of the Glories. I can remember singing on the albums and dreading the times I had to sing solo in front of the others. Dad always made it fun, though, and I can recall him making us all laugh in turn because he wanted to use one of the laughs in one of his songs. Now I am a member of the Glorie Company and enjoy being a part of Dad's team. I have also enjoyed helping him out with little things like when he bought his computer and didn't know how to work it. He let me read through the Amstrad Manual to show him how it worked because he didn't have the time or patience to study it.

What I like best about Dad is his sense of humour. I think he is the best dad ever, and I am proud to be his son.

Joseph (age 15)

Dad is a great laugh. He takes us all to the Sportsdome and we go swimming, and play squash and badminton.

But sometimes Dad works a bit too hard and he gets a bit grumpy, so then we all pray for him and he is better. I think Dad is the greatest.

Daniel (age 13)

All About My Daddy

My daddy is fun and plays games with us. He takes us out to McDonald's, and sometimes he takes us fishing. He teaches the Bible to me, and he is great at doing books, records and tapes and other things, and I think he is a great dad. I love going to the Praise Parties with him and dancing to his music. He loves Joss, Dan, Mummy and me because he tells us a lot, and I love him very much.

Suzy (age 9)

1

Ishmael's Little Angels

'Never work with children or animals' is the old saying. I appreciate that is not a biblical quotation, but I know many Christians who treat it as though it were. In fact, some go to extremes by treating their animals like children, or worse still, treating their children like animals. As for me, well, up until a few years ago the only animals that I really liked were farm animals because of my agricultural background. And I must confess that the reason I liked most of these was because I saw their potential on a nice hot plate to keep the gravy and tomato ketchup company. My reasons for liking children were very different, you will be relieved to hear.

For my younger readers I need to make something very clear: I too was once your age. I know many of you, having seen me, may find that impossible to believe, but I want you to use your imagination. With this in mind, it should also come as no great shock to you that in my early years I learned a lot about children, because, naturally enough, a lot of my friends were children.

But as the years passed by, I got older. I wouldn't say that I put away childish things; I just renamed them. Now they were not called toys; they were called pastimes and hobbies which of course were vital to help me relax and unwind. During this period of my life I never really thought about children much at all. Obviously, they must have been around. But except for visiting the odd Sunday School meeting or going 'coochie coochie coo' to some little baby in a pram outside church (who would invariably cry in horror when he saw my face) they never seemed to be around me.

But then came Irene and, alongside her, love and marriage. Due to being an overworked travelling evangelist there were only four months between our first date and our wedding day. The reason for this was that I had only one free Saturday for the next year. Although this may sound rather speedy, irresponsible, and not the recommended norm, I would also say in our defence that we did know the voice of God, and knew that not only were we meant for each other, but also that God was happy about the date. We also talked it over with our minister, who I am pleased to say was happy about it too.

It was during these very fast-moving weeks preceding the wedding that the subject of children was approached. We quizzed each other on such things as when we would start a family, and how many children we would like to have. It's at this stage that you fail to consider fertility, maturity, the enormous responsibility, and, more to the point, 'when' or even 'if' God wants you to have the little patter of footsteps running around your house.

But we were both of one mind: we wanted to have children, or, more accurately, a child as soon as possible after we got married. I was convinced that this would happen. After all, I had read all the right Christian pre-marriage books, watched the educational films about it on telly, and spent many years on a farm where the facts of life had been revealed to me in graphic detail. Due to my experience, I felt that I was not just Mr Average in these matters.

That is why I was so disappointed and surprised when I discovered that we hadn't conceived on our honeymoon. All sorts of thoughts and questions went through my mind over the next few months. Maybe we were unable to have children. Should we get checked out? How would we cope if it was revealed who the infertile partner was? You know, such 'minor' questions as these. Of course, this was all showing me as I really was: immature, naïve and totally impatient.

It was in our sixth month of connubial bliss that at last Irene became pregnant. Why on earth did it take so long? Never mind, I was over the moon. I remember rushing around telling everyone that I was going to be a dad, and I loved it when everyone came up to me and shook me by the hand then said that lovely word,

'Congratulations.' To this I would reply with the usual old cliché: 'Oh, there was nothing to it.'

In a reasonably short time, the initial euphoria wore off. It may have been because less people were congratulating me, or it may have been the awesome responsibility ahead that was making me feel rather ambivalent about it all. Or was it waking up to the sound of morning sickness in the bathroom every day? Whatever it was, I was becoming a lot more thoughtful about the new little life that was going to come and invade our marriage.

The main problem was, having not had anything to do with babies and children, I had somehow got it into my mind that Irene was going to give birth to a teenager, because this was the age that I was spending all my time working with, and this was the age that I knew most about. I kept thinking about all the fantastic things that my offspring and I could do together, things like touring and concerts. Maybe he or she would, unlike me, really be able to play an instrument and sing. Either way I was convinced that he would be an excellent preacher and that God was going to use him in a far greater way than he had used me.

Being observant, I soon noticed that Irene was getting larger and larger, and being the lovely little, petite, four-foot-ten-inch lady that she is, I feared that there may come a time when she would be as wide as she was tall.

I well remember that long hot summer when she was eight months pregnant. We had gone to the West Country for a holiday, after doing about six weeks of non-stop missions and living in a different house each week. I was beginning to discover just how uncomfortable is must have been for her, carrying around such a weight, tiring quickly, and getting the strangest cravings for the strangest types of food at the strangest times. It was also very embarrassing for her because although we had just celebrated her twenty-first birthday, she looked so young and it could have been misinterpreted as a schoolgirl pregnancy. I remember taking a coach somewhere and the man in the ticket office innocently asked her if she wanted half fare. At this she indignantly took a couple of steps backwards and pointed at the large lump and said, 'No I do not.' I think she should have paid for one-and-a-half.

So although both of us had read much about the effects on the developing body in pregnancy in theory, when it came to the real thing we were learning new and exciting things all the time.

I found it wonderful to hear the little one's heart beating away like a bass drum, but there was always the inevitable fear about babies being deformed or suffering some mental illness. My fear was there because this would have been an area that I knew nothing about, and although I knew there would be no question of my love for my little one, I still, being totally inexperienced in such things, was frightened by the very thought. I should add that in my work with children since then, I have spent a lot of time with some of these little ones that our society has called 'not normal' and they have been some of the most beautiful children I have met. They have the same potential to love, serve, and be used by the Lord Jesus, albeit in different ways, as any child born with a perfect body and mind. What they lack in some areas, they have a double portion of in others.

The big day eventually came, eight months and one week after conception. I was walking up and down the corridor of the maternity hospital like a caged lion along with other expectant fathers. They were smoking to calm down their nerves, while I was praying and trying to keep out of their line of fire as they breathed out the foul-smelling fumes. I had no intention of walking into a sterilised room to see a brand new life, smelling like I'd fallen out of an incinerator.

Soon a large lady dressed in a blue uniform informed me that I could be with my wife during the birth if I wished. This I did, and it was a tremendous experience. I clearly remember being told that I was now the proud owner of a 1973, mint condition son. I remember shouting out, 'Praise the Lord!', and Irene and I praised God for the wonderful gift of this lovely little boy, and for being with Mum during the birth. We were totally elated.

I have always been the sort of person who loves to share good news, especially if it's an 'exclusive'. The phone bill soared as I rang everyone I could think of. most, of course, were over the moon. Some were a little bit more subdued as in my excitement I rang a few wrong numbers and they didn't seem to share my excitement.

I was very proud and within ten days Irene and baby Joseph were released from the hospital. Both arrived home and we began our family as a threesome.

As I mentioned earlier, I had no idea what babies did or how to relate to and communicate with them, so it came as rather a shock to me when I discovered that all this little thing seemed to be able to do was cry, eat, dirty his nappy, and sort of smile if he had wind problems. This was not quite the man of God that I was anticipating.

From that time on, though, I watched with interest as young Joseph developed from crawling to walking, and gurgling to talking, and while this was going on we were blessed with another little baby boy whom we called Daniel.

Having one child was interesting enough, but two children were fascinating. The two boys were as different as Laurel and Hardy. Their personalities and whole way of life seemed totally opposite. Joseph was cool and calm, and as the years went by I could see that he seemed to achieve a lot without really having to try: a natural, you could say. Daniel on the other hand tended to be much more nervous, excitable and through sheer hard work and great effort would attain similar results to that of his older brother. It was also interesting to note that Joseph was never a child that demanded a lot of kisses and cuddles; in fact, from a very young age he seemed to be embarrassed by this. But Daniel with his opposite temperament would always respond to a bit of outward affection.

It puzzled me how two such different children with different needs and qualities could come from one set of parents, but after pondering this for a short while I realised how different Irene and I were and how many of our traits, both good and bad, were being mirrored by our children. When the children were quiet and well behaved people commented how like their mother they were. I can't understand why whenever they were the opposite, it was attributed to good old Dad.

Four years after Daniel, yet another bundle of joy joined the Smale family, this time of the female variety. We decided to call our little girl Suzannah Joy.

21

Just as an aside, never underestimate the turmoil that can be caused by selecting a name. Every parent invests in one of those little books that tells you every conceivable name that mankind has ever chosen to embarrass a child with. At first everyone wants a name from a heroic biblical character and they think that there are plenty to choose from, until they realise that all the best ones have already been pinched by their relations and friends. It seems that the only ones left are Mephibosheth and Ishmael and they can't use the former of these because they'd never remember how to spell it, and the latter, well who in their right mind would want to be landed with a name like that?

We decided on Suzannah, not after the manager of King Herod's household, but because we liked the name. Mind you, the lads, whom I had entitled Joseph Gideon and Daniel Jonathan, were stuck with some of my favourite Bible characters.

As the boys were growing older I found it easier to relate to them, but how would I cope with a little girl? In the past I'd never been very good with the female sex. It was never that I didn't like or respect them; no, it was more that invariably I found them to be stronger characters than their male counterparts or husbands. This usually incensed me to argue with them. In fact, the best disagreements and debates I've ever had have been with the fairer sex, and at the end of our heated verbals either they would end up in tears or I would end up in tears, or they would hit me over the head with their handbags.

Suzy's character was again very different from the boys. She was an extrovert, loved talking and was fearless in front of large audiences; quite a chip off the old block you might say. She was also very caring, sensitive and considerate of others.

I kept my eyes glued to the children as the years passed by, knowing that childhood is short, and I started seeing more and more how God was using them. Joseph's prayers were solid and confident, as he prayed for me to be healed, or had words from the Lord for me, and they came with sincere conviction.

Daniel was always asking questions about life's little enigmas, always seeking to know the real meaning behind truths and statements, never over confident, but always full of energetic excitement and enthusiasm as God began to use him.

Suzy who was a very feminine, frilly, demonstrative little girl went to ballet lessons. Yes, whatever you may have heard, Ishmael does not just enforce bouncing, and on one occasion while she was there, in front of her teacher and the other pupils, she began to sing and dance to a worship song with her hands in the air. After this the amazed tutor and class didn't know what to say, except, 'Thank you Suzy, that was very nice.' She was full of enthusiasm, sharing the good news of the Lord Jesus with any friends she made. All three children had been fully involved with my work before their age reached double numbers.

I have never favoured one child above the other. Just as all three have individual failings and weak-nesses, so too they have wonderful God-given qualities, all unique to them, and I have deliberately taken time over their growing years to discover, pro-mote and encourage these. I don't want them to be replicas of me, or even just fulfilments of my aims and ambitions. I just want them to discover God's will in their separate lives and then go on to see it fulfilled.

If I could leave my little tribe just for a moment, it needs to be said that outside of my rapidly growing family, I still gave very little thought to the younger generation. I had been taught that these were the church of tomorrow, so it was logical to assume that tomorrow would be when I would think of them; but as we all know tomorrow never comes.

For a few years I was pastor of a church in Lancashire. We had a large number of teenagers and a very capable lady looking after the children's work, so again I chose to put all my efforts into the teens and older ones, not being too concerned about what happened to the children as in time they would of course become teenagers and so to my badly educated mind would become of some value in the church. What I failed to realise at the time was that due to attitudes like mine, many of the children never realised their value and hence never stayed in the church long enough to even become teenagers.

Another of my failures was that I was under the impression that if important things had to be done well, it was much quicker and easier to do them yourself rather than train up others. This excluded the children's work as at this time it would not have been on my priority list of important things. But God was about to change my way of thinking.

It was on a Wednesday night when we held our weekly prayer-meeting-cum-Bible-study, and as usual I had arranged that I would unlock the church, set out the chairs, convene the meeting, lead the worship, open in prayer, preach the sermon, give the appeal, close in prayer, make the coffee, do the washing up, then lock up the building. Just the usual things you expect from a one-man ministry.

However on this evening things were not right. I had left home after having a blazing row—sorry, heated disagreement of views—with Irene, and the last thing I felt like doing was going to a meeting, let alone doing all the odd jobs that I had lumbered myself with. But of course I had to be there. I couldn't leave the sheep without a shepherd, even if he was a bad tempered grumpy one, which they probably would have been better off without.

I had a few professional secrets up my sleeve, however, for rare disasters like this. The first dodge was to drop the praise and thanksgiving because you had to look happy for that. The secret was to go straight into some serious gentle worship. With this, people either kept their eyes closed, or those that were looking around either looked miserable or expected to see other worshippers looking miserable. Somehow people seemed to think it was more spiritual and proper to look like this, and with the way I was feeling I had no problem pulling that sort of face. I assumed that people must have thought I looked very worshipful.

But this got nowhere, so dodge number two came into force: I simply told the folk that we would have a time of open prayer. This meant that I could sit down and let them get on with it. At this point I could just about overhear a couple of my deacons whispering things like, 'Pastor isn't his usual self tonight.'

It was at this stage that everyone looked up, including me, as a child started walking to the front of the building. He walked straight into the little wooden box that I was hiding behind, put his hand on my shoulder and started to pray for me. Wow! I don't know what he prayed, but that was unimportant. I immediately leapt to my feet thinking, 'Somebody cares and is not too

25

scared to come and pray for me.' I felt great. In no time at all the old springs had regained their bounce. I apologised to the Lord, and later to Irene, and was back in top gear. It was then that I noticed a deacon flipping through his Bible to see if it was scriptural for a child to lay hands on and pray for his pastor. Without meaning to sound unspiritual, I didn't care. I was just delighted.

This was my first major shake-up as far as children were concerned. God could actually use them. They were not just little things to be seen and not heard. God wanted them to be seen *and* heard. I allowed these thoughts to lie dormant in my mind for a couple of years as I was not quite sure how to develop them.

A few years later I was in a band, and we were doing a tour in Europe of venues where no Christians had gone before. One morning we played in a girls' school to a class full of eleven- to twelve-year-old girls. They were great, although they didn't speak very good English, and by the time we had sung a song through twice, they were joining in as if we were giving a rendition of 'Tulips from Amsterdam'. Then came the evening, and we were playing in a nightclub called the Golden Sunflower which was an open display for everything that is evil and everything you would pray that no child of yours would ever get involved in.

It was then that I noticed a few innocent little faces that I recognised. Yes, there were some of the little girls that we had been singing to earlier that day in school, but now they were being handled by old men before being taken outside to fulfil their duty as prostitutes. It takes a lot to turn my stomach, but this did. I had mixed emotions of tears and rage, and I knew that I would never forget that night.

Soon after this God spoke to me for the first time directly regarding children. He said, 'What you have seen in Holland is already happening in England and it's going to get worse.' He told me that his Spirit had come in power on many people in churches around Britain with no interest in what denomination or stream of house church they came from. He then asked me this question: 'Why is it that this move has failed to touch or influence the children, and why is it that even with all this going on still the drop-off rate of children leaving church in their early teens is as high if not higher than it has ever been?'

I was then led to that well-known scripture in Matthew chapter 18 when the disciples were asking who was to be the greatest in the kingdom of heaven. Jesus had a little child stand in front of the disciples, and told them to learn from him.

That was my commission; not so much to go and teach the children, but more to go and learn from them. For the rest of this book I want to share with you some of my initial discoveries, which are not just theory or an amateur's guide to child psychology, nor is it a book giving all the answers for every individual child. It is really just my first-hand account of what I have learned and experienced by working with and watching these dynamic little troopers.

I hope that this will shake up church leaders, wake up parents and excite our children as they read. I also pray that it will open the eyes of your local church community to see the potential and importance of their children, and also to take their God-given responsibilities seriously.

Matthew 18 states it loud and clear. Jesus said,

> Whoever welcomes a little child like this in my name
> welcomes me. But if anyone causes one of these little
> ones who believe in me to sin, it would be better for
> him to have a large millstone hung around his neck
> and to be drowned in the depths of the sea (vv 5–6).

I would like to share with you a vision my wife Irene
had at Spring Harvest several years ago. I believe,
looking back, that not only was it prophetic, but it was
also a powerful demonstration through the children of
what the future holds for the church.

Every day we would go on a march with the children round the campsite, singing, waving banners and
proclaiming that we were in God's army. As we did
this people would rush out with cameras, and either
stand and watch or join in. It was the highlight of the
day for us as well as the children, and also a very
moving experience as the vast crowd marching drew
vast crowds to watch. Many a time has God's little
army marched through meetings where thousands of
adults have been assembled. Far from causing a dis-
ruption, many of the leaders of these meetings have
told me that as the children arrived a special anointing
came upon the meeting which stayed even after the
children had left.

Here's Irene's vision:

> As I watched the children marching around the
> campsite, the Lord very clearly showed me as they
> began to march in a tight unit together that they were
> following their leaders. I walked alongside them for a
> little way, then stood back. I closed my eyes for a
> moment and could hear their voices above everything

28

else, loudly proclaiming around the buildings. As I stood in the square they came round, and I could see Suzy our daughter at the front line holding hands with a friend. It was Abigail Kendrick. I felt tears in my eyes at the sight of this little army marching for God, and I thought, "Lord, I'm sure there are tears in your eyes watching this." A little boy tripped over, and maybe it was his sister or a friend who helped him up and they held hands and continued to march, catching up with the others. I felt God was saying, "Now, can't you see, this is what I want for my body, my church." I could picture regiments coming together all over the nation; they could be churches, fellowships, anything. They were helping each other put on their armour, and some regiments were already formed with their armour on, linking hands. Loving, caring, looking after each other, encouraging each other and their leaders, they were ready to march.

God said, "Now march, and claim the villages, towns, cities and the nation. Fight for me and my kingdom, because all together we can stand." I can still hear the voices of the children echoing, it was so powerful.

I am sure it is no coincidence that a few years later Abigail's dad was inspired to produce the concept of 'Make Way', encouraging thousands to take to the streets and march round proclaiming the good news of Jesus, and declaring defeat to opposing principalities and powers. This has proved to be one of the most dynamic influences in Britain this decade.

I have already mentioned that I have three children, but I have now discovered that the children of Ishmael are in the tens of thousands. My aim for my wider family is the same as that for my personal family, and that is to see them transformed into the children of God, to be taught their significance, to be given their rightful place in the church, and to be trained to be more than conquerors in a society that has rejected God.

2

Good News for Little Angels

'Please Mummy, don't make me go to that noisy Glorie Company,' screams an insecure little nine-year-old who is making as much fuss as a vegetarian forced to enter a steak house. 'But you must go to Ishmael's meeting. You'll be able to learn all about Jesus and how to become a Christian, and anyway Daddy and I have to go to our meeting so you can't stay with us.'

This is quite a common occurrence, and of course some children are frightened on their first visit to a hall packed with hundreds of other excitable children whom they don't know. I'm sure *I* would be— wouldn't you?

It doesn't help for the child to discover that another reason they must go and be with Ishmael is because the parents couldn't get another babysitter to look after them and Ishmael is a good babysitter who also teaches stories from the Bible. But it goes further. There are so many times when I have found myself in a situation in which I just cannot win. 'I am sorry Madam, but I cannot teach your child all about Jesus and salvation in the next hour. It will take your child that long to settle down and not feel scared, insecure and threatened, and it will take me that long to learn your child's name. But as I do preach on believing for the miraculous and achieving the impossible I will do my best....'

Then come the 'divine' requests which instead of being taken to the Lord, are brought to me. 'I believe that the Lord is going to use you tonight to save my child,' says one, and, 'I know mine will speak in tongues for the first time,' says another, and, 'God is going to anoint you to heal my son's deaf ear tonight,' pipes up a third, and from that moment on comes the flow of great expectations. It's all very flattering, but I know that if I allow that sort of pressure to get to me, I will end up praying for everything and seeing nothing happen. To try and get people to see that they must look to God and not to human beings seems almost as impossible as the miracle they are after.

Don't get me wrong; I love to see parents with great vision for their children. But I wish they could realise that I, like many others, am just a Spirit-filled Christian, and they have the same, or possibly more, access to the Holy Spirit, especially when their prayers involve their own children. So much more could be done in the home, if only they could believe and understand that.

I am convinced that children can become believers at a very early age. I know that some critics would question exactly how much children can understand, but my argument is: How much does anyone of any age really understand when they first become a believer?

I try to picture Mr Average, who almost certainly, if he lives in Britain, no longer comes from a Christian country. The chances are that except for the odd christening, wedding or funeral he has never darkened the door of a darkened building know to him as a church. As far as Christian teaching goes, all he remembers are a few well diluted Bible verses delivered by an agnostic headmaster from his primary school assembly days. And his experience of worship is the odd Sunday evening in front of the telly, accidentally tuning into the wrong channel and ending up watching a few minutes of *Songs of Praise* instead of the programme he was intending to see.

It is a similar process of learning and being re-educated for him as it is for a child. In fact it will probably be easier for the child because he will not have lived as long on this planet, and although he has sinned, he has not had the time to be so tainted by the wickedness around him or to develop the confusion and doubts that adults discover come quite naturally with age.

Yes, children are much more open to being taught, as they, unlike many of their forebears, realise that they have not got all the answers to life's problems. All they have inherited are the unanswered questions.

33

I am thankful to the Lord that the great news of new birth and new life is simple. Some of our evangelists, however, would obviously disagree with me. Having heard some of their so-called simple expositions of 'salvation' I'd say that there was a lot more chance of a camel going sideways through the eye of a needle than any normal pagan understanding a word of what was said.

Thankfully for the unsaved, the words of the Holy Spirit, whose voice they are really hearing, is a lot clearer, more direct, precise and easier to comprehend than most evangelists will ever be. I am sure that at almost any age people can understand what we call the 'ABC of Salvation', and as in the Bible we are all called to share our faith with others, I am convinced that we do not need a degree in theology to tell people how to give their lives back to God.

It is a sad indictment on our church system that both adults and children are being taught how they ought to invite unbelievers along to a 'meeting', rather than being taught how to invite them to know the Lord Jesus. We need to teach both young and old how to pray with their friends and to see them 'saved', and that this is not just the job of the church leader when he gives his Sunday evening appeal.

Although the Holy Spirit will lead individuals to pray in different ways, let me give you some guide-lines on how I personally would pray for children, which may be of some help.

Please bear with me as I run through a few details that I believe to be important for the children to have some knowledge of if they are to understand the basics of becoming a Christian. May I also add that it is not just the words that you say, but the sincerity and

34

simplicity in the way you communicate this message that is going to help the children understand and respond. Obviously the following is a more detailed guide for reference for the older reader. When passing it on to a child one would need to use even simpler words and expressions. And remember that while *we* are doing the evangelising, it is going to be the Holy Spirit who does the saving.

Here we go then; Imagine we are face to face with a child or a crowd of children who are asking how they can become Christians.

Firstly, I am a keen believer in teaching the theology of the Trinity. I believe that God, from the beginning of time till the end of time, exists in three persons: God the Father, God the Son and God the Holy Spirit. Although it is hard for our finite minds to understand, these three persons are not just three separate 'parts' of God; each of the persons is God.

Now, although the Father, Son and Holy Spirit do have different roles to play, they are all involved in bringing about the brand new life of the born-again Christian. So right from the word go I teach the person who I am sharing the good news with just a little bit of how the three persons of the Trinity are involved.

Although some may think that this would sound confusing to children at such an early stage, I have found it to be a lot less confusing than when later on they hear people singing about and praying to various members of the Trinity and our poor young baby Christian hasn't got a clue about what or to whom the people are praying.

Father God

I make it clear that the Bible teaches us that we have all sinned (done things that have hurt God) and fallen short of Father God's glory (not been the kind of people that he created us to be).

So that they don't suspect that I am making things up, I find it a good idea to show them Romans 3:23, so they can see that this is what the Bible teaches. (Please make sure you use a modern translation so that they can understand it.)

I then explain that doing wrong comes naturally, and doing right demands effort. Even if right from when they were tiny no one had taught them to do wrong things, no one needed to; it was one of the few things that they were immediately good at. I remind them that it was not their mums and dads who taught them to do wrong; in fact, most mums and dads spend most of their time struggling to teach them to do right.

I have never had to spend long convincing a child that he is not perfect. Nowadays I have more trouble trying to teach a child self-worth. Let me emphasise that no one has forced them to do wrong actions, have wrong thoughts and say wrong things; they have in fact consciously or subconsciously chosen to do these things for themselves.

Do they realise how it breaks Father God's heart when we choose to do things that, deep down, we know upset him? I then ask the child to say sorry for the things that come to mind, and if he can think of one specific thing he continually does that upsets Father God, he should not only say sorry for this but should ask God to give him the strength to stop doing that thing completely.

Although I may not use such a long word as repentance, that is what I know God wants to see: a complete change of mind, and an attitude that says they are going to stop living just to please themselves and start living to please God.

The Lord Jesus, God's Son

If they believe in the Lord Jesus Christ they will be saved. Scriptural references: Acts 21, and many many more.

I try not to take anything for granted, and knowing that some have been taught nothing in their homes about the Lord Jesus, and taught wrong concepts and ideas in their schools, I try to explain in a few simple sentences who Jesus is.

I begin by saying that the world was in a mess. Satan (the devil) who is against God and all that is good, but nowhere near as powerful as God, fooled many into following him and his evil ways, just as he does today. But Father God so loved people that even though they were not being obedient to him he sent his only Son Jesus down to earth to show them how good life could be if we lived in a way that pleased him.

I go into quite a bit of detail about how the so-called religious people of the time couldn't cope with the Lord Jesus because he showed them up for the wicked people they really were. I also explain that they rigged up a false trial, that they were happy to watch Jesus being beaten up, and that even as he suffered excruciating pain as he was nailed to a wooden cross they still felt no guilt or shame.

Then I ask the children, 'How would you feel if someone had done that to you when you were innocent? I imagine you would have been shouting things back at them, telling them how unfair they were being. But the Lord Jesus didn't act like that. In fact, he was just the opposite. He loved those who were killing him, and he asked his Father to forgive them because they didn't understand what they were doing.'

Then comes the hardest, yet most important, detail to explain. In the Old Testament animals were a substitute for man, and that is why they were sacrificed to take away the wrong things that man had done. But here on the cross Jesus was the perfect Lamb of God, and as he was being sacrificed to deal with all man's wickedness—past, present and future—even Father God couldn't look at his Son as he carried in his body all mankind's sin.

He didn't deserve to die; we do. Jesus was our substitute and he paid the death penalty for our wrong-doing.

As Satan saw Jesus dying on the cross he was thrilled because he thought that he had destroyed God's Son. But it was then that with his fading breath Jesus shouted out, 'It is finished,' which was not a cry of defeat but a cry of victory. It literally meant, 'My work is completed.' Satan, sin and death need no longer be man's destiny. Jesus through his suffering has unlocked the gates of heaven and offers life without end for those who believe in him.

Being physically dead, Jesus was buried like other men in a tomb, but in those days it was more like a cave and had a big stone rolled over the entrance. But after three days an angel of God rolled away the big stone and when people looked inside there was no dead body to be found because Jesus had come back to life. Over a short while he showed himself to many, even telling them to touch him to prove that he was not a ghost but the real Jesus who had risen from the dead.

This is not a story or a fable; this is the truth. To become a Christian it is important to believe that these things really did happen.

And finally, this means little if we don't allow God to come into our lives and change us.

The Holy Spirit

I continue by saying that Jesus, being in human body like you and me, could only be in one place at one time, so Jesus said that he was going to go back and be with his Father until the time was right for him to come back and wind up man's time on earth for good.

He also said that he wouldn't leave us by ourselves. He would send his Holy Spirit, who, being Spirit, could be everywhere and in everyone at the same time, and that if we invited his Spirit to come and live in our lives, he would not only start changing us so that we could be more like the Lord Jesus, but he would also give us power to live out our lives on earth in a way that pleases God.

After this, it is important to have just a short time where the children can reflect upon what they have heard, pray, and also be encouraged to speak out loud and thank God that he has not only heard their prayers but has also already begun to answer them. Teaching them to speak out loud is again a good starting point; you want them in time to be unafraid to speak out and pray in public.

Although this may sound wordy and too simplistic in parts for the older Christian, I hope you get the point that I am making. Just as children and adults have varying degrees of intelligence, so their understanding will vary, but if we present the biblical way of salvation in a way that they can understand, the Holy Spirit will reveal the truth, whatever their mental or physical age.

When a little baby is born into this world it knows nothing and has nearly everything to learn. It is the same when someone is reborn into the family of God and becomes a Christian; they too begin a new life and have nearly everything to learn. The day our miraculous new life begins, we know that a change has taken place—to use a Bible quotation, 'We have passed from death to life'—but it is going to take a little while before we start to understand what exactly has happened. The Christian life is not a one-off experience where we are filled with all knowledge and become instantly perfect; once born we start to develop and grow, and it is as we mature that we start to realise what exactly has happened to us.

It infuriates me when parents see me a few hours later and say that they can see no change in their child, or worse still, when they confront the child after a slight misdemeanour and use such worlds as, 'Call yourself a Christian?' Internal change is instant, but habits of a lifetime, even of a short lifetime, may take a little while to die.

That is the straightforward bit, which I share with either an individual or a crowd. This may give some clue to the parent who is not sure what to say to their seeking child and is waiting for an itinerant children's evangelist to come along and do the work for them. Expect to see your children become Christians at an early age, and also expect to be the ones who will be introducing them to Jesus and praying with them for their salvation.

This will often happen quite naturally at bath times or bed times as you are together. Allow times for questions to flow, especially during or after a bedtime Bible story or while you're enjoying the relaxed atmosphere of lunch after your Sunday meeting. Remember that the actual moment a child decides to become a Christian, whether in the home or in a meeting, is so often a culmination of many little 'chats' that you have been having together. It is important to keep sowing.

Please don't feel that you will be doing us children's workers out of a job if it's you that helps them to become Christians and not us. I often feel that I am doing *you* out of a job. Ephesians 6:4 says, 'Fathers, do not exasperate your children; instead, bring them up in the training and instruction of the Lord.' Okay Mums and Dads, get on with it. Why leave all the blessings to us? You deserve a few of them yourselves.

Moving on from the individual to the larger group, I usually feel it right to give those to whom God is speaking a chance to respond to him in a public way. It's not that I want to embarrass them; it's just that once they have made a stand in front of their friends, declaring that they want to serve God, they do seem a lot stronger for it and, understandably, it is not so hard for them when they start to tell other friends what Jesus means to them. But any sort of appeal involving children has to be thought through.

We evangelists love to quote numbers. It looks very impressive in a news letter when 'hundreds come to the front'. As well as giving us a sense of security, it also lets others know that we are doing our job well.

Personally, numbers have never impressed me, and since working with children I have noticed just how inaccurate headhunters or handcounters can be.

A short while ago I was in a meeting with about 750 eight- to eleven-year-olds, and after some fun and worship I presented the good news of Jesus to them. While still in quite an emotional atmosphere, I appealed to all those who wanted to give their lives to Jesus for the very first time to stand up and come to the front. Before anyone moved I repeated two more times that it was only for those who had never done this before. The minute I finished speaking, about 350 squeezed their way up to the front, and as I stood on the stage and saw the enormous mass of little heads in front of me, the optimist would have thought that revival had broken out, while the pessimist would have thought that it was pure emotionalism. The truth was it was neither.

As we took the children to one side to pray for them, we discovered that the words I had used in my appeal had changed by the time they had reached these young ears. 'I came forward to keep my friend company,' said one. 'I wanted Ishmael's autograph,' said another. One even commented that we had given him a little booklet the year before, but he feared that when he lost this, he may also have lost his salvation, so he thought he had better come forward and get another one.

This is one of the reasons why we get the children to write down on a piece of paper a prayer of thanks to God for what he has done in their lives, for then, and only then, do we start to get a realistic idea of what has actually been happening.

On this evening, out of the 350 initial responders, about 100 children genuinely became Christians for the first time.

This was confirmed by the number of parents I have seen subsequently who have told me of a dramatic change in their children's lives since that evening. That is exciting. As for the rest of the children who responded, I praise God for them too for a couple of reasons.

The first is, we had a chance to pray for them and it's always a great privilege to pray into these little one's lives. Secondly, it's great that they are not frightened to stand up and walk to the front of a meeting. The church will be much healthier if when these young ones reach adulthood they are still as open to respond. I believe that a lot of adults miss out because they are too embarrassed to respond openly when God speaks to them.

There are, of course, many other ways of finding out those who genuinely would like to be prayed with or who wish to know more. The most common is the 'hands up, stay where you are' appeal. The only trouble I've personally found with this is that while the Spirit of God is moving in their lives we encourage those who are already Christians to worship the Lord, and of course for many of them nowadays their most natural expression of worship involves raising their hands. It looks great from the front, but unless you are good with your words of knowledge, it is going to be a bit of a job to sort out the sheep from the would-be sheep.

I suppose the most accurate means I have found for finding those who want to become Christians is this, and it involves two things.

What you don't do is offer any 'bait' or reward such as a little book, because most children would love a free book, even if once they have seen how boring it is, it ends its life as a paper aeroplane or swept up with the rubbish on the floor. You may still give a book to those who respond afterwards, but you don't advertise the fact that you are giving them away during the appeal.

What you can also do is, when you have finished sharing the good news with them, just say, 'For those who want to give their lives to Jesus, see me at the end of the meeting.' You only need to say this once. Then do something quite opposite like a real bouncy action song to completely break the emotional atmosphere that you have built up.

I do believe that if the Spirit of God is really moving in a child's life, amid everything that may follow they will remember to come and see you after the meeting. I have proved this to be true. This is ideal for the smaller children's meeting which is held at regular intervals, where you have already built up a good relationship with your children, but weekly appeals become repetitious.

Finally, a few hints for when you are leading an evangelisticmeeting:

(1) For those who have responded, it is good to get them to pray a prayer after you. It is important that you keep it short and speak slowly. I remember the first time that I did this I spoke so quickly and with such long sentences that the children could not keep up with me, nor could they remember the sentence that I told them to repeat. Worse than that, neither could I.

(2) Never under any circumstances take children out to another room to pray for them. Non-Christian parents are very suspicious of Christians nowadays— understandably so, because of all the adverse press that we have been given. Be open, let people see what you are doing, and if they are nearby, invite them to join you as you pray.

(3) When a child from a non-Christian background gives his life to Christ, someone needs to go and talk it through with the parents. Don't just leave it to the child to explain, as he may accidentally say all sorts of things that will horrify the parents. Send round your best evangelist; a great opportunity!

(4) Don't forget to teach the children that what they have received they need to share. Also teach them how to share it. They will be better than any schools workers as they get alongside friends of their own age. Oversee them, but don't feel that you have to be for ever walking behind them to see if they are saying the right words and doing it the way you would do it. They probably won't be. They are children and it is quite normal for them to say things in a childish way. If we have trained them well they will portray God's heart, if not our words, and there will not only be a lot more labourers going into the harvest field, but there will also be a lot more crops coming into the barn. Yes, God has put no age limit on his workers and neither should we.

Here are some prayers by children, written down in their own words on how they became Christians:

Sacha: O God, will you come and live in me? Thank you for the things you have done for me. I will be a good girl more.

Joanna: I love the Lord Jesus and know that he will take me through all times, hard, difficult and easy. I have taken him into my heart and he is lots of fun.

Anon: Dear Lord, thank you for coming into my life, and thank you that I can really know that your power is in me.

Anon: I feel very very happy that I have become a Christian. This is a very big day for me, God.

Anon: Dear Lord, thank you for your Son and letting him die for us. Thank you for Jesus. Amen.

Ruth: Thank you for cleaning my life and making it clean. I thank you, Lord, and I will put my trust in you. I love you, Lord.

Anon: Lord, I want to have my heart and your heart.

Anon: Dear God, we thank you that you died on the cross so all our sins, illnesses and problems could be solved. We thank you again, Lord, in Jesus' name.

Barbara: Thank you, God, that I have just become a Christian with you.

Anon: I feel that God has put new life into me. I now feel new. I feel changed.

Emma: Dear Jesus, thank you for helping me make up my mind. I have now truly become a Christian. I love you. Thank you.

Anon: Dear Lord, I am sorry for the wrong things I have done. Please forgive me and come into my life. Help me to do more good than wrong.

Rachel: Jesus has changed my life. He has forgiven my sins. I will love him for evermore.

Anon: Thank you, Lord, for entering into my life. It is the best thing you have ever done for me. Thank you.

Hannah: I've just entered into God's life, and he's entered into mine.

Anon: God took all the bad and dirt out of me and I felt good.

Josey: I feel now as though I have become a real Christian; as if a light has lit up in me.

Anon: God has now made me a Christian, and I am very happy that he has managed to do this for me.

Anon: Lord, I feel new because you have come into my heart. I want to thank you, and please help me to stay a strong Christian and help me not to tail off.

Anon: Dear heavenly Father, please come and live in me. I am very sorry that I have sinned and gone my own way. In Jesus' name.

Anon: God has changed my heart and we are going to live together in peace.

3

If I Speak in the Tongues of Men and of Angels

Ladies and gentlemen, in the right corner we have the Reformed, conservative evangelical, who has grave doubts about such things as the baptism in the Holy Spirit and the gifts of the Holy Spirit, especially speaking in other tongues. He says that he is solid, mature and not made up of froth and bubble, and agrees with the apostle Paul who once said, 'Tongues will pass away.' He believes that the greatest gift is love, especially for those who think the same way he does. In his mind not only is he convinced that certain supernatural gifts did pass away a couple of thousand years ago, but he would have been highly delighted if those who differ from his opinion had passed away at the same time.

And in the left corner, ladies and gentlemen, is his opponent, the renewed, revived and restored charismatic. He is not only Spirit-filled, but believes that the church should be known for its supernatural signs and wonders. He too agrees with the apostle Paul, who once said, 'I would that you would all speak in tongues.' He believes that love is not a gift, but the greatest fruit of the Spirit, and in practice loves his gifts more than the people that he is offending. He is convinced that the Reformed conservative evangelical won't put up much of a fight, because not only does he lack power, but he also lacks life because he comes from what he would describe as a 'dead' church.

This is the so-called classic confrontation, which to my mind is probably the biggest time waster and red herring of the century. Personally, I believe in being baptised in the Spirit. I feel honoured that God should choose to share his supernatural gifts with me, and of course I teach people how the gifts can be of benefit to them and the kingdom. I also however have a lot of good friends who don't share my views, and I respect them as being very close to God. I know it breaks God's heart when we lose love for each other and just get involved in endless hours of swopping scriptures and argument.

Often people come up to me saying that they don't particularly like the way I do things, and they often disagree with some of the things I say, but they praise God for me and for the way he is using me to help change others' lives. Now that is what I call an honest compliment.

It's healthy to have our own thoughts and ideas which are founded on our backgrounds, our interpretation of Scripture, and even our personalities. The biggest danger to the church is people not being allowed to think for themselves and hold their own opinions. They end up just becoming little clones of their leadership team or denomination. Thank God for our diversity. It is God's intention that being part of the same family we can still have a real love for each other that is stronger than any of our disagreements. And the term 'dead church' is a contradiction in terms, as the real church of our Lord Jesus Christ will never die.

But sadly, even after saying all that, the issue of the baptism in the Holy Spirit and his gifts is still an emotive one and one which causes many to separate and split from even their closest friends.

'Charismatic' and 'Reformed' are words which mean little; it is the life that speaks so much louder than the words. I know so many folk who would not claim to be charismatic who are wonderfully used by God, and so many that claim to be charismatic who are not only an embarrassment but will be judged for turning peoples' hearts away from God.

I belong to an army, and I am not just an individual soldier seeking recognition. I may use different tactics and weapons from others, but I'm proud of being associated with any who are living their lives with one aim: to please their Commander. Not everyone, though, is quite so pleased about being associated with me!

My personal experience is that some are filled to overflowing with the Holy Spirit when they become Christians, and as I pray for people nowadays I would expect that to be the norm. But others, including myself for many reasons—ignorance being the greatest—have experienced a baptism of power at a later stage.

Praising God in new unlearnt languages seemed so often to be part of being drenched in the Holy Spirit in the New Testament, and again I believe that those who are overflowing with the Spirit of God have been given the ability to do just this. But because God would never force us to use any of his gifts, we need to ask him for them and also to understand that receiving them will require some participation from us, even if it is just opening our mouths and speaking out in faith.

Just a few words of advice here for those who may be seeking this wonderful experience. Firstly, don't look at the gift, look at the Giver; don't think about speaking in tongues, think about praising Jesus.

Secondly, don't be in fear that what you receive may come from the evil one or even be of your own making. Believe Matthew chapter seven when Jesus says how his Father in heaven will give good gifts to those who ask him. Remember, our heavenly Father is much more powerful than the evil one and you and me, and he wants us to have the best.

Thirdly, don't panic if you don't feel much different or nothing seems to happen while you are being prayed for. You have asked in faith, and it has been given. You will notice the new power in your life once you start witnessing to others, and you will probably start praising in tongues when you are relaxed and by yourself.

Fourthly, the more you praise in new tongues, the more fluent the language or languages seem to become, so without making an exhibition of yourself, keep praising God at every opportunity.

The day of 'heavy-handed' people, putting their heavy hands on your head and shaking it until you speak in tongues, is thankfully disappearing. Those who pray for others must realise it is wrong to try and force one of God's gifts onto someone. It is as the word says, 'a gift from God', and only he can give it.

Finally, you must always bear in mind that God won't use your gift *for* you; he gave it to you for *you* to use, so use it whenever he leads you to and use it wisely.

Now I've mentioned tongues first, not so much because it is the initial evidence, although it is certainly the evidence that most people experience first. Paul says in 1 Corinthians 14:4 that speaking in tongues edifies us; in other words, as we praise God with this gift we actually get built up. We also realise that we have been filled with power from on high so that we can go and give out more to others. This in time, will drain us, so it makes sense that time needs to be spent praising in tongues so that we can restoke our boilers, or get plugged back into the power source for a recharge. We may only get baptised in the Holy Spirit once, but we do need constant refilling with the Holy Spirit.

My own pesonal testimony is that although I had been prayed with to be baptised in the Holy Spirit, and felt supernatural power fill me, I was not released in praising in new tongues until some time later. On reflection, the biggest disappointment for me was some of the unhelpful advice I was given by some of the leading Pentecostals of the day. As I questioned them about this gift and told them I would love to use it to glorify God, they would just tell me not to worry about it and that God would give it to me in his time. The truth was that they could not be bothered, or they were far too busy dealing with important problems to spare time for my burning questions and confusion.

One rainy night on the Sussex coast I had just returned from a meeting where it seemed that everyone, including Irene my wife, was using this gift and consequently they all seemed to be on a different level of praise than me. I was still struggling with the good old English language, incessantly repeating such expressive but earthly words as 'Hallelujah', Praise the Lord' and of course a few 'Glory's' while everyone else around me seemed to be taken up to the heavenlies, shouting out God-given phrases. Now I know that the words are not all-important—it's what your heart is feeling that matters to God—but I'm afraid at that moment this was no consolation to me. I just felt the odd one out, rather like a cabbage in a Christmas tree plantation. Maybe you have also felt this way. It's weird how in such a large meeting with so many brothers and sisters who love you, it is possible to feel so alone and inadequate.

That night as we approached the front door of our flat, I told Irene that I wasn't coming home until God gave me this gift. Thankfully she could see my desperation and said that she would be waiting up and praying for me till I received it.

Marching up and down the promenade, I was shouting to God and asking him why he was withholding this gift from me. I paid no attention to the nocturnal dog walkers who passed by on the other side and understandably considered me to be some sort of nutcase. Even the rain, which had by now managed to soak through to my underwear, was no distraction. In fact, I paid no attention to anything, not even to God. I guess he knew that I needed to let off steam and he allowed me to do just that.

After a long time I was still shouting, but not in English any more. I am guessing, but I think that I must have been shouting in tongues for fifteen minutes without realising it. Boy, did I feel good when I eventually started listening to what I was saying. I still feel good as I reflect on that time. A wonderful warmth covered me all over on that cold, wet night, and I spent ages just dancing around praising God for this wonderful gift that he had given me.

Please don't get me wrong. I am not recommending this as the normal way to be released in tongues (though I can guess that no one has ever described me as normal), but maybe you can see now why I get a little annoyed when Christians look down on this gift by saying it is the least of the gifts, insinuating that it is of little use and that while seeking the 'higher' gifts this little one can be ignored. I believe that every gift from God is priceless and so valuable to you and me that it is close to blasphemy for us to downgrade any of them.

Perhaps this shows you a little of why worshipping in tongues is very precious to me. Nowadays it is invaluable, after having been criticised, hurt, or drained after ministry, just to fix my mind on Jesus and worship him in this way. It is indescribable—well, in English anyway.

So what is the big controversy? Well, we don't need to make it one. When folk come up to me and say that it isn't for them, fine, I must respect their viewpoint. But on the other hand if I say to them that it is for me, they must also respect mine. Nowadays I refuse to argue about it; as I mentioned earlier, it is more important for me to stay in good fellowship with people than to win a theological argument. After all, at the end of the day it is going to be the Holy Spirit who will change people's minds on issues like these, not me.

So that is that; everybody's happy. Well no, not really! Most would find this highly acceptable for adults, but once children are mentioned nearly everyone's viewpoint changes.

Biblically, I don't see why it should. I can find no reference to the above being for adults only, and surely if we are talking about this being a supernatural gift from God, God would not allow children to have it if it was bad for them or even if there was the remotest chance of there being any adverse effect.

The main problem that Christians have with this concept is that it has never really been part of their thinking. With all the talk of renewal that is spreading throughout the world, it seems that the only area of our church not to be touched is our children's work. We are still telling the same, sometimes unbiblical, stories in the same way, and singing the same old songs, with the same expectations as our great great great (ad infinitum) grandparents had. The only difference today is the results, which sadly prove that even less children remain at church after they have become teenagers.

I knew that God had something new and refreshing for our children as well as for the rest of the church, and I was convinced that part of this was to introduce

56

them to God, the Holy Spirit. In most churches all they had known was the Father, the Son and Holy Scripture.

Again I repeat, scripturally we are given no age limits for most of the things that we as Christians need to learn and experience. The prophet Joel prophesies that God will pour out his Spirit on 'all' people, and surely that 'all' must include children. I also find from Scripture that the Lord Jesus delivered a little girl that had an evil spirit. If a child is capable of being demon possessed, this shows me that children are involved in spiritual warfare. That is why I not only desire to see that my children are Spirit-filled, but I want them to have everything that Jesus has provided for them, both for their defence and to help them attack the evil one. I'm convinced that if the church equipped and trained children for battle, we could save a lot of their suffering and falling away which I definitely do not see as the normal 'phase' through which they must pass as they move into adolescence. If we choose to place them in state schools, which so often can be demonic breeding grounds, we owe it to them to prepare them for the onslaughts and temptations that they are going to face.

More important that this we are shown in the Bible that there are things which are harmful, and we should shelter, protect and guard our children from them. How can any genuine Christian put the Holy Spirit in this category?

We must also realise that we are talking about a supernatural gift. Our finite minds, whether adult or child, will not be able to understand it fully. That is why books like 1 Corinthians go into such detail, giving all sorts of instructions to help us. These are so simple and really just common sense. Dare I say that even a child could understand it? It is certainly a lot more straightforward than teaching the meaning of baptism, what happens when we take communion, or the principles behind tithing and giving, which most of us would see as a priority in our children's education.

For the reader who knows little about me, I ought to explain that as well as preaching, my main means of communication is through music. A few years ago, I decided to make a record all about this subject which hopefully children could relate to. It was a story album about some little characters called Glories, and in very simple terms looked at the Holy Spirit and his gifts or presents in a way that most ages could understand.

I had decided to use both my sister's children and my children on the album, and was pleased when the Lord showed me that he wanted these children to experience what they were singing about before they actually went in to do the recording.

I'll never forget that evening in my front room. Without me even praying for them, they were individually and spontaneously filled with the Holy Spirit and started praising God in other tongues. I was also taught an important lesson when I went to rebuke one of my little nieces who was giggling and I thought was being flippant. I was about to walk over to her and have a gentle word in her ear when God stopped me and told me to say nothing. He reminded me that she was a little child who loved giggling, and that I should not expect my adult, intense, heavy way of doing things to be imitated or copied by children. Then, as I looked at this little girl again, it was like seeing her with a new set of eyes. Without instruction she had raised her hands in the air, and I saw that she was totally absorbed in worshipping her Lord. Their praise went on for ages and seemed to grow louder and louder as they ignored me, forgot about their own inhibitions and concentrated on the Lord.

Since then I have been privileged to pray for hundreds of children and see them become Christians and filled with the Holy Spirit.

Yes, I made my mistakes. Sometimes I got a bit carried away in a meeting and encouraged the children to go further in gifts of the Holy Spirit than their leaders had gone. Quite rightly, I got my knuckles rapped. But just as the children were learning, so was I.

I don't take all the blame for upsetting people, however. I was in one church and had just finished preaching in the Family Service when a mother brought her nine-year-old daughter up to see me. She explained that God had been speaking to the little girl and she asked if I would pray with her to become a Christian. I told the mother that I would love to and then invited her to stay with me while I prayed, but she felt that for one reason or another she would rather not and walked off to the back of the hall.

I explained a little bit more about what becoming a Christian was to this little girl and then got her simply to repeat a short prayer after me, similar to the prayer I described in the last chapter. After she had done this, I told her to start thanking God in her own words for hearing and answering her prayers. This was when the trouble started.

This church had not been encouraged to use the supernatural gifts, so I had been very careful not to overstep my brief and deliberately avoided mentioning them. Then this little girl, without any instruction from me, started praising God not in English but in tongues, and her little face was radiant.

I must admit that even I was surprised, but not half as surprised as her mum. She must have had good ears because she came flying down from the back of the hall, shouting at me and asking me what I had been teaching her daughter. She continued, before whisking the poor little girl out, 'I only wanted her to become a Christian; I didn't want her to have this.'

I've had this happen several times, the most embarrassing time being when a whole Brownie pack started praising God in new languages and the Brown Owl, who was not quite as wise as her position might suggest, flew out of the hall, her feathers very ruffled.

I have learned my lessons, but I have also learned that I cannot give the Holy Spirit restrictions. As Scripture says, 'The wind blows whereever it pleases. You hear its sound but you cannot tell where it comes from, or where it is going. So it is with everyone born of the Spirit.'

As long as it is the Holy Spirit doing the work and not Ishmael, I can't go wrong...well, in his eyes anyway.

Here are just some of the hundreds of prayers from children in connection with the Holy Spirit:

Jonathan: I have spoken in tongues for the first time and asked for healing. Praise the Lord. (His father had read it and wrote underneath it: Dad praises with you, Jonathan.)

Samantha: I was filled with the Holy Spirit and laughter. It's great. (P.S. I can't stop laughing.)

T Macintyre: (in very wobbly handwriting): Today I was filled with the Holy Spirit and felt the power of God come in me. I was shaking afterwards.

Anon: I am a double Christian.

E Wilson: I have been refilled with the Holy Spirit and know I have been forgiven for all I've done wrong and know that God loves me and I'm special.

Fuzzy: (we do teach the children how to pray over others): Today I prayed for Andy who's been filled with the Holy Spirit, and it's really blessed me.

Helen: Thanks, God, for filling me with fun, laughter and the Holy Spirit all over again. It was great.

Suzanna: At first nothing happened, then the words of God just came flowing out. Praise the Lord. I'm born again.

Helen: (many receive healing as they open up to God): I have spoken in tongues to God and my hand has been healed. Praise the Lord. I love him.

Anon: As I prayed, my lips and hands started to tremble, then I just started talking in tongues.

Adrian: (not satisfied with just saying it, he felt he needed to write down what he was saying. Please forgive my interpretation of his written tongue, but I couldn't read the writing very easily): *Ich Kann in zungen reclen holclem Herrn.* I can speak in tongues. Praise the Lord.

Anon: Lord, please fill me with your power so I can sing your praises.

Andrew: The Lord filled me with his power and I felt an entirely different person.

Anon: Lord, you gave me confidence tonight. Boy, did I need it. I could never accept your Holy Spirit before, I was too shy.

Johanne: Dear Lord, I have had a proper talk with you. When the prayer was over I felt happy, and I feel as if my whole body can float up to you.

Anon: Holy Spirit, thank you for entering my life and helping me to do my exercises. (Very interesting!)

Kathryn: I believe that God has given me his power so that I can witness to my schoolfriends.

Anon: Thank you, God, for recharging my batteries, and I praise and worship you. I just don't know how to say how much I love you.

Anon: The Lord God has filled me with his Spirit so that I can go into the world and preach the Gospel.

Billy: Dear Lord, fill me with your Holy Spirit. Fill me with power to win my battles, in Jesus' name.

Anon: Lord Jesus, thank you for filling me to over-flowing, Lord, 'cause deep down I felt empty. Lord, I praise you.

Anon: Thank you, you gave me a refill.

Carolyn: I felt warm with the power of God flowing through me again. I go to church, but it is boring, but now filled with God's power I want to cry with happiness.

4

Angels Move in Where Prophets Fear to Tread

I must confess, when I was a young child the main thing I looked forward to at Christmas was not the celebration of the birth of the Lord Jesus, nor was it the roast turkey, potatoes, sprouts, peas and cranberry sauce for Christmas dinner. I'm ashamed to say that it was not even the chance to give to others. No, it was the thought of receiving all those wonderful presents that was the highlight of my Christmas.

It is also honest to say that although I was not a selfish child, when I received a gift that had my name on it, my initial thought was that it was just for me and not to be shared with others. After all, they had received their own gifts, so why should I share mine with them?

Within a week or two, though, my attitudes changed and as the gift had received my undivided attention for quite a while, it was now not only time to let other people enjoy sharing it, but it was also time to see what they had got and to begin to share their treasured possessions.

A few years later, my priorities changed. Celebrating Jesus' birth had, of course, gone to the top of my list, but the other major change was I had now discovered that it was as much fun hunting around and finding gifts I knew would light up other people's faces as it was opening up the ones that were given to me.

Even more years passed, and nowadays I know the Lord Jesus better than I ever did. Now I've learned not just to celebrate his birth at Christmas, but I am thankful for him coming on to this earth all year round.

Instead of getting the exciting toys I used to get, all I receive now are the boringly useful and practical items; you know, socks, pants and handkerchiefs, and most of these tend to be the wrong size, or the wrong colour, or duplicates of a gift given by someone else. I know I sound totally ungrateful, and of course I am exaggerating to get over the point that nowadays I much prefer giving to receiving. I get more satisfaction seeing someone's face as they open their presents, than I do opening mine.

What has all this got to do with anything? Well, let me try and explain. When children are first filled with the Holy Spirit and released in the gift of tongues, it becomes like a new toy to them. They are able to do the impossible by speaking in a language that they have never learned. They didn't have to spend many hours reciting and practising like they may have done at school during their French and German lessons.

In a powerful way they have discovered that by knowing a supernatural God, they are now able to do supernatural things. Not only is this gift going to build them up—it will also be a great outlet for expressing their praise and worship.

As with the child and the Christmas present, in the first few weeks the gift they have been given is likely to become the be-all-and-end-all. It will be all they talk about: tongues for breakfast, tongues for dinner and tongues for tea, and there will still be a few things to say about it at supper time. That is quite normal, because understandably it has been a very exciting and unusual discovery.

The Bible instructs us that tongues of praise can be used any time, and this is again why Paul gives us guidelines on how and when to use them in public so that things can be done decently and in order. But our young enthusiast in those early days will not understand or even particularly want to understand Paul's wise advice.

There will be times when they go way over the top, either by using this gift at inappropriate times or even by looking down on others who have yet to receive it. At this stage, our friends who are not sure about this gift and its relevance for today are usually completely put off, and put it down as being a strange experience especially for weirdos or fanatics.

Now a child needs to be taught that this is only the first step along a very exciting road, but the problem comes when their leaders have failed to let God develop them in other areas, because then the whole church is stuck at a tongues dead end. Unless they move on they will become self-indulgent and of little use not only to the church universal but, even more importantly, to those who are not Christians. 'Since you are eager to have spiritual gifts, try to excel in gifts that build up the church' (1 Corinthians 14:12).

I cannot underline the fact enough times that the main reasons the disciples were filled with the Holy Spirit on the Day of Pentecost were that they could give glory to Jesus, and that they might have the power to go out and supernaturally influence people, revealing that not only is the Lord Jesus alive but he is also all-powerful.

Here we come to the second stage of my Christmas illustration. Not only is it exciting to receive gifts, but it's also exciting to give them away.

I would now like to share with you how I have taught children the importance of some of the other supernatural gifts, and how they can bless others as they use them. This does not belittle the wonderful gift of tongues which they have received; it just moves them on to show them that there is life beyond tongues.

The gift that is most closely related to tongues is the interpretation of tongues, which I personally believe to be a gift that has somehow gone missing and has ended up being completely mixed up with prophecy.

1 Corinthians 14:2–3 tells us: 'For anyone who speaks in a tongue does not speak to men but to God. Indeed no-one understands him; he utters mysteries with his spirit. But everyone who prophesies speaks to

men for their strengthening, encouragement and comfort.'

Further on in verse 29, we are told what has been shared as a prophecy should be carefully weighed up by others, but nowhere are we told to weigh up an interpretation of a tongue.

I know that although the gifts do overlap, interpretation of tongues and prophecy are two distinctly different gifts, but what is the difference? I discovered the answer 'out of the mouths of children' the first time I decided to do a children's houseparty.

Having never arranged anything like this before, I was greener than an under-ripe tomato. I decided to seek advice from a much more experienced children's organisation. Understandably, they did seem rather anxious about what I was experiencing and seeing as I explained to them how children were being supernaturally touched by God. The main advice that they gave me for my weekend was to have plenty of games and recreation as children love these. Now again it's confession time because, although I had spent numerous evenings with children doing what we called 'Praise Parties' which were all age celebrations, I had never played any games. I had tried to make whatever I taught fun, and considered other activities to be unnecessary and time wasting.

Having listened to this advice, I did arrange for a sports programme on the Saturday afternoon. As the weekend progressed I was amazed by the insatiable appetite that these children had for learning about Scripture. Apart from that Saturday afternoon, I had crammed the weekend with seminars on the Holy Spirit, which they soaked up like ink on blotting paper.

It wasn't long before it was me who needed a break and also a coffee, so I told them to go and get some fresh air. After a few minutes, though, I couldn't believe my eyes; they had all returned and were eagerly waiting for more, and I'd only had one mouthful of my coffee and half a biscuit. They exhausted me, they were draining every bit of information from me and they were excitedly coming back for more.

Not normal, you may say. I tend to agree with you. When I was younger and went to some of these weekends, the only reason I was able to survive the teaching sessions was that I knew that in an hour or so it would be over and then I would either have the chance to play football or acquaint myself with the members of the fairer sex. If I was lucky, it would be both.

But was I normal or just downright unspiritual, and would I have been different if I'd had the opportunity to hear about the exciting relevant truths that these children were learning about now?

At one of these sessions I was teaching what the Bible says about the gift of interpretation of tongues. I have always been of the opinion that not only tongues spoken in public, but also tongues spoken in private, can be interpreted, as I had done this myself many times and found it beneficial. I could never understand why people would say that praise tongues didn't warrant interpretation. Why on earth not?

Anyway, after the theory had been taught, then came the practical. We started to pray, and the children started praying in tongues. It was then that others spoke out and gave the interpretations. It was lovely to hear the ones who had given the tongues comment on how amazing it was that someone else had been able to put into English exactly what they were feeling, and also to see how the interpretation was so much more of a blessing to all of us than the tongues had been. Well, it's common sense really, because now of course we understood what was being said.

But then came the most interesting revelation.

I had not taught these young ones how to interpret tongues; I simply told them to ask the Holy Spirit if he had something that he wanted to say through them, and if the answer was yes then to get on and speak it.

The scripture that I shared with you earlier stated that when we speak in tongues we speak to God, not to men, and these unconditioned children's interpretations were to God, not to men.

Suddenly it all made sense; the missing gift had been found. If tongues is Godward and an interpretation is translating that tongue into English so we can all understand it, it goes without saying that an interpretation is Godward as well. If a tongue is speaking to God, how can the interpretation be speaking to men? If a tongue is speaking to our Father, how can an interpretation start with the words 'my children' or 'the Lord would say'? For years I believe that many of us have followed a tongue with a prophecy and not waited to hear the interpretation.

How much easier it is now to understand why Scripture teaches these as two separate gifts. A prophecy must be weighed up and judged to make sure that it really is God speaking to man, but an interpretation does not need to pass through the same scrutiny as it is man using a supernatural gift to pray to God.

Let me explain how varied these children's interpretations were.

Some, as in Acts 1, were simply praising God, but it was as though their English language had been expanded to the nth degree. They were praising, using poetic phrases and similies that were laced with the majesty of the Psalms of old. These were not just prayers of praise, these were anointed words of thanksgiving that none of the children could have possibly given without the supernatural input of the Holy Spirit.

But not all were praise; some were crying out to the Lord for help, and again you could hear that both tongue and interpretation were not joyful and ecstatic, but were sombre and serious, unquestionably Spirit-inspired as these children would not have known how to pray with such depth and feeling.

So can the church be built up by an interpretation as much as a prophecy? You'd better believe it!

After the tongue, to hear someone sharing with God their feelings under supernatural anointing not only has a great influence on those around, but it also often paves the way for God to respond and speak to us through the prophetic word.

So to sum up, I am not saying that it's impossible to have an interpretation where God speaks to man, and the church has been misguided for all these years. No, it would be wrong to be so categorical, but what I *would* say is that we need to define these two gifts, even if it is only for the sake of teaching our children.

As the Bible defines prophecy as God speaking to man, maybe a few words about children and this gift would be appropriate.

A few common sense facts first. We all know that not everyone who is used in prophecy is automatically a prophet, just as not everyone who has witnessed to people is necessarily an evangelist. Some prophecies are predictive, but to be genuine God-given prophecies they must, of course, come true. The majority of today's prophecies are summed up in Corinthians again, when Paul says that everyone who prophesies speaks to men for their strengthening, encouragement and comfort. It is worth remembering that they don't hack down and destroy.

I expect we have all heard some wild prophecies, and maybe in our less experienced years we have even given some. It is important that we don't become lone rangers and always have godly men and women around us to either confirm what we are saying or who are honest enough to tell us when we are up the creek.

It is silly, if not untruthful, to prefix a prayer with 'thus saith the Lord' or 'God says' for a few reasons, but before I give them to you just listen to these funny yet embarrassing stories about people who have used this prefix to their so-called prophecy.

One said, 'Thus saith the Lord, as I said to my servant Moses...or was it Abraham...?'

Another laid hands on an individual and began, 'Thus saith the Lord, oh dear, I have forgotten thy name.'

And a final one that was given the day after a church had held a barn dance: 'Thus saith the Lord, I was with you at your barn dance last night, yea I enjoyed being with you, in fact I haven't enjoyed myself so much since I parted the Red Sea....'

Clangers? I'll say! Once you've had one of those spoken to you, or over you, it is quite understandable why this sort of prophet would not be accepted in his own town, or in anyone else's.

Here are a few reasons why it is unhelpful to prefix what God wants to say through you with the words 'thus saith the Lord'.

Firstly, in any prophetic statement, very rarely is it 100 per cent God speaking. Parts of it may be, but so often the human influence is very detectable, especially when it seems to go on for a long while and it has that nice refined, well-rehearsed ending. No wonder the preacher in Ecclesiastes tells us to let our words be few.

Secondly, it is unnecessary to tag these phrases on. Some may consider that it adds clout to what is being said, or wakes people up to the fact that a prophecy is on the way, but if it is a supernaturally anointed word, people will sense God's authority as it is spoken.

Thirdly, if it turns out that it was not a prophecy that was shared, but some human feeling that was sincerely imparted, not only will the prophecy be false, but its proclaimer could be judged as a liar as well.

Children need to be taught these facts, and as they are learning to hear and know the voice of God, be prepared for a few human errors. Mistakes will be made, but remember, not all mistakes are sin and we do learn by them. Sin is when God tells us to say something and we don't say it—it is disobedience— not when we say something with pure motives but get it wrong. Don't be too hard, just lovingly train up and educate them in a way that they can understand. Remember, if you are too harsh on them, or leave them in any way looking silly, you can gaurantee it will take them years before they are willing to speak out again, if ever.

Let me share with you two visions that Jonathan, a young boy of five, had: He saw two rabbits in a hutch, a mother and a baby. The mother was glossy and well-fed, but the baby was thin and scraggy. The humans had been feeding the mother but not the baby, and at night it would try to escape to look for food.

After weighing this up, the parents took this as a word to themselves and the church. They had been feeding the adults spiritually but neglecting the children, and so the children would look elsewhere for what they needed.

He also described two men: a man who loved and a man who hated. The man who hated built a wall between them. The man who loved planted seeds and plants on his side, but the other man would sneak around at night, steal them and plant them on his side.

They shared this vision with their church, as they felt it applied to the evangelism they had just begun, and warned them the enemy would use people in the town to steal the seeds they had planted in people's lives.

Jonathan's older brother, Simon, had a vision at one of our Weekendaways: He saw a rugby team playing a match. One of the team had the ball, but would not pass it on to the rest of the team and held onto it himself.

His father shared this vision at a leaders' conference along with other words and visions. It applied to a leader who was organising a major project against all advice and was holding it to himself instead of being part of a team.

At one of my meetings I got all the leaders to kneel on the floor, and told the children that if God had given them anything to say into our lives to come and share it with us. Out they came one at a time and spoke with the accuracy of an arrow hitting the bull's eye. Unlike adults, they don't waffle or wrap up what they have to say in nice polite sentences; they simply say it as it is, short and sweet and straight to the point. I do not recommend this exercise for the faint of heart or those who are not prepared to hear the truth about themselves!

5

Ministering Angels

Dear Ishmael,

We want to tell you what happened when you visited our town last year, what the Lord has done for our eldest son Tobie and to thank you for your ministry.

Tobie had been having fits very regularly, often daily, for the previous year and a half. At his worst he had eleven in one day and he could be unconscious for up to three quarters of an hour and usually was quite unaware of what he had been doing for many minutes before each fit. He was beginning to lose great chunks of his life.

Of course, we, his family, friends and church, were worried. He underwent many tests, was regularly hospitalised, passed from consultant to consultant and still no cause was confirmed.

My husband and I had been sure at the beginning that God would heal Tobie, probably by using the medical profession. Many people prayed regularly for him, but over the months our family prayers became less hopeful, less trusting. After all, if God was going to heal him, why was he continuing to have fits? Knowing that God's timespan and ours are very different was no comfort. Sometimes I felt Jesus to be very far away. He was letting me down. I was building worldly barriers between us.

Tobie had been a thoughtful child, and he had witnessed and often spoken of the difference that had occurred in the family when my husband and I had asked Jesus into our hearts a few years earlier. Following a week with friends at a Christian holiday, where he continued to have fits, Tobie's own faith became very strong, very alive, and he was filled with the Holy Spirit. He ministered to others and he prayed in a way new to me, such an intimate way with the Lord, a sure way, knowing he was being heard, that the Lord was his loving Father who was listening to this thirteen year old, and would answer his prayer.

I think that Tobie prayed for others at this time rather than himself. Seeing him reassured me in my faith, but we still found it hard to pray for his healing with any conviction.

Then you came to our town. The Lord used you that day to minister to Tobie. Tobie asked the Lord whether he was going to heal him or not, and as he closed his eyes "a massive yellow YES" was all he could see. His father and an older friend stood and prayed with him, and Tobie knew he was healed. He told us, and although we rejoiced and thanked the

Lord, we continued to have our doubts. But what worldly-wise, God-ignorant children we are. Of course Tobie was healed, and has come on this past year in strength and grace, continuing a wonderful relationship with the Lord. He had one final fit, and was able to tell the consultant that he would not need the hospital any more.

This is just one of the many exciting letters I have received, but sadly my success rate in healing is far from 100 per cent. Once I was in a large room with hundreds of children sitting in front of me from every conceivable background. My subject was 'God still heals those who are ill today'. I wanted to find out what the children already knew about the subject, so I asked them to put their hands up if they had ever seen people who were sick being prayed for. A blanket of hands went up.

I then asked if any of them had ever prayed for a sick person and through their prayers had seen people healed. Understandably, the response was nowhere near as large, but there were still quite a few who responded.

I then asked if any of them would like to come out to the front and tell us all how God had used them in this area so together we could praise God for what he had done through them, and I chose a couple to come and join me. One of these was a young lad who looked very serious, so I brought him over to the microphone and asked him who he had prayed for, to which he quickly replied, 'My Dad', I then asked what had been the matter with his father, expecting to be told that maybe he had had flu or back trouble or something similar. However the little boy said that he had cancer. There was a visible gasp around the hall as I could sense the children getting very excited at what was about to be said. I certainly was very excited. I then said to the little chap, 'And how is your dad now?', waiting with baited breath and convinced that I knew what his reply would be. After a short pause the little boy answered, 'He is dead.'

Silence fell all around the hall. Even yours truly couldn't think of anything to follow that. I did find it interesting to note, however, that the child was not sad. He had obviously seen his dad suffering so much that the greatest healing he could in fact receive, and presumably the best answer to his prayer, was for his dad to go and be with the Lord Jesus.

I have always been brought up to believe that we worship a God who heals. My own father has a piece of shrapnel lodged so close to his brain that surgeons could not operate on it and predicted at best, terrible regular headaches and at worst, I dread to think. But Dad rejected their human wisdom and obeyed James chapter 5 by calling together some of the leaders of the church to pray over him and to anoint his head with oil. It must be noted, though, that some of these leaders knew nothing about healing and had never dreamed of being involved in this sort of thing. Well, here we are years later. Dad still has the metal in his head, but he is not suffering from any of the predicted side effects.

Having in later years also been involved in traditional Pentecostalism, I had learned good and not so good things about healing. As a pastor it was always my duty to pray for those who needed prayer, but in all honesty it was a miracle that anyone got healed (please excuse the pun). I really didn't have a clue as to how to pray over people, and my faith was not even hope. Many times, as I prayed, my mind was either a blank or thinking about what song I would follow this part of the service with.

I was never disappointed, though, because I never really expected anything to happen. Most of the old folk would mutter something after I had prayed for them like, 'Thank you, Pastor, I think I feel a bit better now,' and those that were obviously no better, I would advise to just keep looking to the Lord.

It was a few years later that I had the tremendous privilege and opportunity to meet and become good friends with such great men of faith as Colin Urquhart, Ian Andrews, Roger Forster and Roger Price, and I spent many hours not only listening to what they had to say on the subject, but also watching how they went about praying for people.

At first I tried to copy their methods, but this turned out to be disastrous as they were all unique and none of them did things in the same way. Then I started to glean a bit from each of them which seemed to be appropriate for me, and at the same time as doing this, I started spending more time with the Lord to find out how he wanted to use me in this area.

As well as learning from these and other great men and women, I also had a lot to learn about healing from children.

At another of my Weekendaways, again with about thirty-five children, I started sharing with them about healing. I wanted to show them how important this gift was, because about a third of the four gospels are accounts of healings. I went on to explain that although Jesus was the greatest Preacher the world will ever know, he knew what people were like and that, as well as hearing words, they needed to see supernatural signs and wonders. I pointed out that Jesus didn't just heal people to get a crowd around to hear him preach. No, he healed people because he didn't like seeing them suffering and wanted to see them made well.

I told them how Jesus had no set routine. In Matthew 8 he touched Peter's mother-in-law and also used spittle for the blind man. In Matthew 12 he spoke to the man with the withered hand. In John 9 he prepared a plaster for the blind beggar, and the woman with the haemorrhage touched him in Matthew 9. Jesus never wanted us to copy a method.

I also made it clear that we could not heal anybody; it was God who was going to do the healing, but faith is required. Faith, I discovered, was a word that all of the children had heard before, but none were quite sure what it meant. I found the best way to describe faith in simple terms was to quote and try to explain Hebrews 11, 'Now faith is being sure of what we hope for and certain of what we do not see' (v 1).

I do make it very clear, though, that faith is not just believing that something impossible will happen. I have met a lot of people who are believing God for something, but it's something that God doesn't want them to have so they won't get it. We must understand that faith comes from hearing the voice of God, and when God tells you that something is going to happen, you not only believe it but it is as though you actually see it take place and start thanking him for it before it actually does.

In healing, I encourage the children before they pray for someone to ask God if he wants to heal that person, or if there is something stopping them from getting healed which may need to be dealt with first.

We may be able to bluff our way through with adults, but you can't fool children. If we teach that all who are prayed for are instantly healed, the child will believe us. But should they pray for someone and healing doesn't take place they immediately become shattered and disillusioned and may even wonder if Jesus has let them down. Their belief and faith take a nose dive. That is why we must be honest in our teaching.

It may come as a surprise to you that although I have seen thousands of children healed, I have also seen many who have not been healed. I need to explain why this is.

John 5 tells us about a paralysed man who was healed but he was warned to go away and sin no more unless something worse happened to him. Deliberate sin is one reason. Unbelief is another reason. Matthew 13 tells us that Jesus could not do many miracles, because of the people's lack of faith. 2 Corinthians talks about Paul's thorn in the flesh, which some say was his wife. I personally believe that it was some kind of physical or mental ailment which as he says remained with him to keep him humble.

Another important part of Scripture is 1 Corinthians 11. Talking about breaking of bread, it says, 'Anyone who eats and drinks without recognising the body of the Lord eats and drinks judgment on himself. That is why many among you are weak and sick, and a number of you have fallen asleep' (vv 29–30).' And then there is good old Job, whom God allowed to go through all sorts of physical horrors to test his faith.

There are many more reasons why we sometimes need to discover the root cause of the problem. Fear could be the cause. I remember for some time Irene's arm was aching badly and she asked me to pray for it. I asked the Lord what was causing this discomfort and he showed me that she had a certain fear in her life which was the problem. As I prayed against this fear she felt a sensation like water draining down her arm and out through her fingertips. That trouble has never recurred to this day.

A little girl had warts and scars on her hand that she wanted God to heal. As she asked God why they were there he told her that she had a strong fear of catching any contagious illness that happened to be around. Through this immense fear, she usually caught it. As she prayed to God and asked him to take that fear away, not only did she know that the fear had gone, but she also saw the warts and scars immediately disappear from her hand. I'll never forget seeing her overjoyed mother afterwards who just could not believe what she was seeing.

We must also realise that unless we are around when the Lord Jesus returns, we all have a time to die. Bodies do grow old and deteriorate. Some do choose to over-indulge and eat too much, or maybe smoke, which helps speed up the process. Some literally take no thought for their bodies and give them no exercise, which again could give us a shorter term on this planet. Whatever the facts are, one day our limited time down here will be up.

I seriously believe that we sometimes do not see people healed because we are praying that they should stay down here, but the Lord has planned it that it is their time to join him. Please don't get me wrong, I would still pray that they can be released from pain, but as has happened many times before when false prophecies are given about somebody living who then dies, this is not only devastating for their loved ones, but it is in no way glorifying to God. Get the point that I am making: before we pray wild prayers of hope, someone needs to have a talk with Father.

The disciples asked the Lord Jesus to teach them how to pray, and we need to teach the children how to pray over someone for healing.

Let me illustrate this by telling you about a young girl who went to pray for an older lady in a family service that I was attending. The lady had nasal trouble and the medical profession had not been able to provide any cure for her.

I told this girl to pray with a voice of authority, a bit like a sergeant major, as she was on the King's business. I told her in the meeting simply to speak to the ailment and tell it that it did not belong in this lady's life and therefore in the name of Jesus it must go and leave her alone. She then should pray that the healing power of Jesus would come upon this lady. Well, this she did and with such a loud voice that everyone nearly jumped out of their skin and turned around in amazement. She didn't wait to find out if the lady was healed; the possibility of anything but that happening never occurred to her.

It took a few minutes before the lady leapt to her feet and with a smile that beamed, shouted out that for the first time for ages she could breathe normally. I saw the leaders of that church about six months after that and they confirmed to me that the lady had had no trouble since that evening.

As important as praying for others will always be, I was also learning how important it was to teach the children how to pray for themselves.

I was a classic migraine sufferer and I knew that because I allowed myself to get anxious and tense, I often brought it upon myself. I went to Roger Price to pray for my healing, but before he prayed for me, he spoke to the Lord and said that the Lord wanted me to be part of my own healing. He told me that I would be given a warning when the attack was about to start and then I should go somewhere quietly and pray to God that the pain would go.

That was not what I really wanted to hear. I thought that Roger would pray over me and I would be instantly healed, as I had seen happen to other people earlier that evening. But I listened to what he said and thought I would try it and see what happened.

It was fantastic. The first time it took me a few hours of prayer to get rid of the pain, but that was better than the twenty-four hours that it normally took and this was without using the powerful pain-killing drugs that I had got used to. The next attack it took less time, and the next even less, and even the attacks became weaker and weaker, until nowadays even when I do feel stress, the attacks are so short and mild that I hardly notice them. My faith was being built up.

The level of faith, both in the individual and the local fellowship, needs to be rising continually. Remember, low levels of faith can seriously inhibit healing just as it did for Jesus in Nazareth.

I was amazed when I heard about the faith of two little girls in one of our meetings a short while ago. The children had separated off into pairs to pray for various things to be healed when one of my workers noticed one of these little girls taking her sock and shoe off. When my worker asked her what she was doing she replied that she wanted to see her bare foot so that they both could watch her verrucas disappear as they prayed. My leader backed off a bit but continued to watch them, and sure enough with comparatively little surprise showing on their faces they saw every verruca instantly vanish. It proved to be no big deal for them; as it would have been more of a miracle if Jesus didn't heal them than if he did as they knew that this was what he wanted to do.

I must add that I am not into the name it, claim it, everything on demand syndrome. Deep down I am a realist. I teach the children that we do not have the right to tell God that we want something done and we want it now or else. He does not want spoilt brats, he wants loving children. I do however make it very clear that once God has said he is going to heal, he definitely will do it, but he will also do it in his time. Don't panic if it's not in your time and don't give up believing that God will do it; God is as good as his word.

As part of their worship, I often get the children to reach out to the Lord and receive healing for themselves, and they do. This doesn't stop them praying for others, but it does build up their faith, strengthen them, and it gets them used to hearing and knowing the voice of God.

Don't teach children to despise or belittle other types of healing, such as through doctors and medics. They do of course have their place, although I personally believe that we should never teach our children to rely upon them or drugs at the expense of God the Healer. Encourage them to go to God first. Prayer practice, before medical practice.

At our large week-long events working with large numbers of children, we like to have a nurse or first-aid person in the team. A short while ago a ten year old was playing a ball game outdoors on the concrete when she fell and severely cut her leg. Our nurse saw that the cut would need stitches, and the little girl was crying so much and obviously in great pain. The first thing our nurse did was cover it with a piece of lint, and then along with several others she prayed. After a short while the blood-soaked cloth was lifted up—and there underneath was...nothing.

God had squeezed the skin back together again without leaving a scar, or the slightest mark. The little girl jumped up, said, 'Thank you, God,' then ran back to carry on with her game. The only evidence of any sort of accident was a blood-soaked lint.

Don't forget to teach children the difference between God's supernatural healing and the evil deceptions of the confusingly-named 'Christian Spritualist healings' which they will be hearing about at school. The evil one tries his best to imitate God, but the best he can offer anyone through his couterfeit so-called healings are sadness and confusion.

Never let the counterfeit put you off teaching the real truth. Remember, if children are given good honest instruction on the gifts of healing—not just successes, but also our failures—because of their simple faith and their wonderful ability to hear God's voice clearly, many miraculous signs and wonders will take place through them.

Here is a selection of some of the hundreds of accounts from children who have been healed. Nothing is too minor or too major for God to heal. None of these are made up or exaggerated; these are the children's own words.

Sue: God has healed the deafness in my right ear; it has got a tingly feeling. [Children often feel sensations when God begins healing.]

Anon: God has healed my eyes and I don't need to wear glasses. [I remember this little chap. His glasses were taken off as he was being prayed for and when he went to put them on again his eyes had improved so considerably that they were way out of focus with his spectacles on. From that moment on his sight continued to improve.]

Anon: God has healed me of epilepsy. I knew it, I can feel it.

Ruth: I had crooked teeth. The Lord has started to move them into the right places.

Anon: When we were singing I felt my right kidney grow. I haven't had one since I was two and half.

Joanne: The Lord has healed me of a bloodshot eye.

Anon: I have been healed. My eyes had a squint and it has gone.

Anon: I say thank you to God for making me able to hear through my left ear.

Melanie: My verrucas have gone. Praise the Lord.

Daniel: God has restored my right little finger back to its former position. Thank God the Healer.

Anon: God has healed my athletes foot which I have had for nearly four years.

Helen: Thank you, Jesus, for healing my sore throat. I knew God had healed me by a tingling sensation in my throat and also a burning feeling.

Laura: I have had permanent tonsilitis for about two years and that has given me very bad headaches and dizziness. When I was prayed for the pain went nearly unbearable, but suddenly the pain disappeared. I will see my surgeon in October and I know there will be no sign of tonsilitis. Praise God.

Becky: I've had glandular fever, and the after-effects have still continued to make me tired. The Lord has healed me from this and I praise God.

Jonathan: I have been healed of eczema. Eczema is a skin disease which makes you want to scratch yourself and you end up covered in scabs. It also dries up your skin. Thank you, Jesus.

Rachel: Three weeks ago I fell off a wall and fractured my wrist. Tonight the Lord healed it, praise the Lord.

Anon: I was healed from an illness that made me go to the toilet a lot.

Anon: I have been having stomach trouble for a few years now. I haven't had it all the time. It comes and goes just as Ishmael had said. I received the words of the Lord and I felt as if a volcano was erupting. Thank you Lord.

Matthew: The Lord has made me sure that he will heal my thumb so I can clap freely.

Rebekah: I was healed of my dyslexia.

Tim: God healed my verrucas, all six of them. Praise the Lord.

Mel: God has healed my periodic pains.

Finally, a few interesting ones.

Jenny: I have been healed from a blocked nose and I think I can speak in tongues. [Could this mean that if you are having trouble getting this gift all you need is to buy a handkerchief?]

Becky: I have got some warts on my fingers and sometimes I get a very bad pain in my tummy and ankle. Lord, I ask you to bless them. [Bless...but hopefully not multiply.]

A Tiny: Jesus has started to heal me of my clod. [I think that was meant to spell cold.]

Anon: Jesus healed me of my ears.

Anon: My nan has Parkinson's disease. Please let her die happily and may she have a good time in her last year. [Note, this is under the healing chapter, not the prophecy one.]

Anon: Jesus healed my toe. My toe was only this big: |————|. Now it is this big: |——————————|. [Grown by at least a foot is my guess.]

6

Suffer Little Angels

Do you remember the days when children used to be little bundles of fun and energy? When you walked past a playground the noise was deafening as you tried to dodge past the flying footballs, tennis balls, the pretend mummies with their dollies, little chaps with cars, trains and aeroplanes and little soldiers, cowboys and Indians, all rushing around everywhere. Children were action-packed and so often self-entertaining.

They were effervescent, bubbly personalities who would never stand if they could jump, would never walk if they could skip, and would never talk if they could sing or shout.

But the pressures of our time and generation are gradually squeezing out childhood and replacing it with premature maturity brought about by unanswerable situations when young minds are forced to make adult decisions and try to cope with adult responsibilities. A primary school near our home recently had to send two little girls home who were genuinely suffering from depression. When I was a child I didn't even know what the word meant, let alone what it was to suffer from such a terrible plight.

Children are repeatedly told that they should grow up, but they are rarely given a Christian role model to follow. Some tell their children that they should be like Jesus, but as children learn about the Lord's love and perfection and see so few human beings around who even vaguely resemble what they read about in the Bible, it seems an impossible task, even though in the long term they do want to grow to be more like him.

Maybe they should copy their leaders. It's exciting to know that there are a great number of godly men and women who are sold out for Jesus, but it would be no exaggeration to say that there are very few who the children would find approachable and be able to call their friend, unless of course the leader happened to be some relative.

To a child, leaders can be like 'the management' who are above everyone else, and the only time these people in high places would actually take any notice of them would be if they were visiting their homes. Then, along with the dog, they may get the customary pat on the head, or if they had done something wrong in the church they would get a verbal if not physical pat on another part of their anatomy.

It is also worth mentioning that in my experience, as I have observed the leader/flock relationship, few leaders find they are able to form a real mutual friendship with the non-leaders and their wives because position will not allow it, and certainly the non-leaders and wives find it hard to relax with them so, realistically speaking, what hope have the children got?

Of course, it's obvious, a child should copy his parents. Yes, that is very true. But are we good examples? I will say more about this in a moment.

Therefore, what do they do? Well, the answer is painfully obvious: the same as the unbelieving child. they tend just to try and imitate their favourite hero of the time. Their walls are not covered with men and women of God; they are more often than not filled with pictures of people who at best could be described as idols who worship themselves, living for fame, money and things to excite their bodies—in fact, all the things we hope our child will not get involved in.

Just a part of growing up, some say; all children have to go through this stage. I am sorry, but I am not convinced of that. However, I *am* convinced that we need more Christian heroes involved in every walk of life, so our children do have national and international names that they can look up to and who we wouldn't mind them imitating, knowing that what they are imitating, at worst, is harmless and at best, encourages them to display Christian values in their lives.

Let us take a look at some of the pressures that are affecting our 'little troopers'.

The place where they will be most influenced in life is the home, and the major problem that they are going to have to cope with is feeling unloved or rejected.

As a pastor I used to have the idea that the more meetings you had, the more spiritual your congregation would be. Therefore I deliberately made sure that every night of the week was filled, and it did look good to see a church notice board which was crammed with events. I was also under the impression that a sign of an individual's spiritual state was their loyalty and commitment to God which was portrayed by their loyalty and commitment to church meetings. So it was only right to think that those who managed to get to every meeting were in fact my spiritual giants.

It was only when I visited their homes that I discovered that nothing could be further from the truth. With either Mum or Dad out each night of the week, there was no time for any relationships or friendships inside the family and all sorts of dissension and rows were taking place. But it was the child who seemed to be showing the most strain. It was easy to see that even the most placid of children were either becoming aggressive or moody, and always seemed to be seeking attention.

As a so-called full-time Christian worker I had forgotten that Dad had probably left his house before the children were even up, and by the time he returned home, either the children were well involved with their homework, or Dad was too tired to talk to anybody. All he felt like doing was sitting by the fire with his dinner on his lap and cheering himself up by watching the news. Then he would have his shower and was off to the meeting. Saturdays and Sundays were no better for the children, as Saturdays were spent working on the car, garden, house or worse still shopping, and of course Sundays had more meetings than the rest of the week put together.

But leaders' children surely cannot feel rejected. After all, Dad is usually self-employed and as his hours are so flexible, he is able to choose how much time is spent with his family. Nothing could be further from the truth. It's because his time is flexible that a leader who usually enjoys his job cannot work out what is work and what is pleasure. A leader has a built-in insecurity that unless ministered to, could easily take all the joy out of him. It tells him that his congregation are always watching him to see that he is not just sitting at home reading his Bible but he is actually an investment of the tithes and offerings, however small, that they put into the collection plate each week. I remember during my pastoral stint one old chap who made it very clear that because he was putting a certain sum into the offering plate each week, he not only expected me to visit him each week, but also should he need anything, I should be available twenty-four hours a day to rush over to his house because, after all, he was paying for my services (if you'll excuse the pun).

A leader can be a bit like a learner driver who is taking a driving test. He not only has to be an overworked busy man, but he has to go out of his way to make sure that everyone else sees that he is the most active man in the church. Everything must be exaggerated, but at what cost?

So often his home shows this lifestyle. I have walked into numerous leaders' houses and found the most undisciplined children that I have ever seen. More than once I have walked into a house where a little child, who I have never met before, comes up and starts hitting and kicking me. Dad and Mum smile in embarrassment saying what a lively little fellow their son is and how he loves to have his bit of fun. The only trouble is, when they try to drag him off me, the child pays absolutely no attention to them and continues taking his rejection out on me. This is one of those cases where the father is so super-spiritual that he has only read in the book af Acts about laying on of hands; he has somehow ignored the many Scriptures which talk about another sort of laying on of hands which, if lovingly applied to a child, will be a sign of caring and not neglect.

Don't get me wrong, I am not expecting children to just sit down and smile as if butter wouldn't melt in their mouths. But spoilt and naughty children need discipline and hurting children need help, and we must be careful that we don't get these two mixed up.

I had just finished doing a service in one church when one of the children's workers came rushing up to me in a state of frenzy, saying, 'Quick, there is a child at the back of the hall who needs deliverance.' I told her to calm down and explain herself. Pointing at some poor bedraggled lady a few feet away she told me that this lady had just become a Christian, but her husband was very involved in witchcraft. She continued again, building up steam: 'On the floor is their son, who is uncontrollable, possessed, and has just been swearing at me. Now could you please come with me and deliver him.' I glanced at the poor mum who just stood there and hadn't got a clue what was going on.

I told the over-zealous children's worker to stay with the mum and I would go and see the boy. It wasn't hard to find him as he was sitting by himself, looking very afraid. I sat down next to him and the minute I did so he looked at me, eyes blazing with a mixture of fear and anger, and shouted, 'You won't get anything out of me.' I smiled and reassured him that I did not want anything out of him, I had just come to see him to be friendly and to find out if he had enjoyed the meeting we had just had.

Suddenly his defences went down. I put my hand on his shoulder and started to talk to him all about music, instruments and anything really that he wanted to share, and I saw that this was just a normal little boy with a lot of hurts who needed a lot of love. If anyone was in need of deliverance it was the children's worker, not this little chap.

A short while ago, we were organising a series of meetings and in the mornings we had various activities going on to teach the children how to be more creative. One of my helpers asked me to have a word with another young lad who was causing a lot of trouble and not wanting to get involved with anything.

I saw him standing in the corner with an anorak over his head and, calling him by his name, I took him for a little walk and had a talk with him.

I asked what was wrong, to which he replied that he hated drama. In fact, he hated everything. I spent a little while longer with him and then I asked him the question again: what was wrong? This time his answer was different. He told me that everyone kept saying the word 'father', and this week his Mum and Dad had separated and every time he heard the word 'father' he felt like crying. At this point he did start crying. And for the rest of the time we had the meetings, we were not only able to talk to the boy's mother, but also to understand why the little chap was behaving like he was. We were able to pray with him and explain about a heavenly Father who would never leave him or forsake him.

In order to deal with a problem, we need to find out the root cause of why the child is behaving like he is. Girls tend to react differently when they are suffering from rejection. They are either very shy and never open up, or more usually they are the ones who hang around you, cling onto you and won't let you go.

I must repeat again that this feeling of rejection is very common in Christian children.

Scripture teaches that we must seek first God's kingdom and his righteousness, but then I believe comes our family, not meetings or even ministries. Our families are our first congregation and responsibility, and we have no right to be in any form of leadership if we cannot lead our own family. 1 Timothy 3:5 says, 'If anyone does not know how to manage his own family, how can he take care of God's church?' If that is not enough, we also hear in 1 Timothy 5:8, 'If anyone does not provide for his relatives, and especially for his immediate family he has denied the faith and is worse than an unbeliever.'

Our children are on loan to us from God; we only have them in our immediate care for a very short time. That is why it must be one of our priorities to spend time with them, and although praying with them and teaching them from the Bible is vital, so is playing with them and really building a friendship with them which will last long after they have left home. They need to feel that they are special to you and not just something tagged onto the 'any other business' of the church agenda.

Remember, they find a lot of security in your home so don't make it a hotel or a hospital. Most houses have a family room, where you may sit, talk, play games or watch the television together. When you arrange an evening in with the children, make them your priority.

Children need to feel wanted. I must say that not all feelings of rejection are brought about by neglectful parents. Sometimes, for various reasons, the child chooses to want to feel unloved. This is another story, which again I have seen the power of prayer change.

Children can feel rejection at a very young age, and if it is not dealt with it will not only lead to massive problems in later life, but also extremely serious consequences while they are still young. There was an article in the *Times* some while ago, entitled 'Life and Death of A Child in Despair'. It went as follows:

> One profoundly disturbing American study published in 1984 looked at sixteen pre-school children, aged two-and-a-half to five, referred to a psychiatric clinic for suicidal behaviour. Thirteen of them had made multiple attempts. Most of the children were abused, neglected or unwanted by their parents. The others had experienced loss of a parent through divorce or death. Child psychiatrists said they expressed combinations of profound feelings of abandonment, yearning for reunion, despair and hope of remedying their painful lot. It went on to say that most children who deliberately harm themselves don't want to die, but simply 'to make people aware how bad they are feeling'.

True, these may be from non-Christian homes, but every year I am meeting more and more children with horror stories who come from Christian homes and who have seen their Mums and Dads separate. Some have bruises on their bodies where they have been assaulted, and some have stories of how they have been sexually abused.

We are not called to be psychologists, but we do need to get answers and learn how to counsel these little ones.

Just a few hints on how we deal with some of these problems.

Firstly, in connection with our leaders, we must contact the parents or parent with custody. They need to know what we have discovered and give us permission to pray with their child. They usually agree, as they can see how difficult and unmanageable their child has become, and they want to see change. It also gives a chance for the leaders to counsel and pray for parents who will be needy people too.

Secondly, we need trust and respect from the child. This may not take very long because although he may have been hurt by those he trusts, he is so crying out to be loved that he will recognise genuine affection and concern.

Thirdly, go into some detail about God the Father and tell him that he loves him, cares for him and even understands how he feels. Explain that he does not want him to be hurt, and even though things have taken place in his life where no person can help, God cannot only help but can heal every situation.

Lastly, ask the child if you can pray for him. Tell him that the rejection he is feeling is not really part of him as he belongs to God, and go on to say that when you pray for him you are going to tell these feelings to leave him alone. Then with a gentle voice take authority in Jesus' name, break the hold of rejection and pray into that life the love of Father God, asking Father to fill any gaps in the little one's life that may have occurred.

Yes, the child has to receive this prayer, but in my experience the vast majority of them do. Some of my most exciting moments have been as I have prayed over children in this way and seen an unbearable burden lifted off the child, then seen a wonderful transformation of character take place as God has come in and done what only he can do.

With all this talk about ministry, let me stress once again that many children do not require this. All children are sometimes a little rebellious—maybe to God, or maybe to their parents—and what may be required is correction and discipline, not prayer.

My brother-in-law lived in an end-of-terrace house where the back gate led into a passageway which ran between his house and the next and led to a quiet cul-de-sac. As he was standing in his gateway, his two-year-old daughter wandered out and started walking towards the road. My brother-in-law had instructed her that she could play in the passageway but must go no further than the end where it met the pavement. The little girl thoroughly understood the rules and proceeded to walk to the very end of the passageway to the edge of where the forbidden zone began. At this point she stopped and turned around and looked at her dad with a 'shall I, shan't I' sort of look which only a little girl of this age knows how to give.

Dad called out again and reminded her that she must go no further. My little neice turned around, took another look at her dad and another look at the road, decided to make a dash for it, then off she set as fast as her little legs would carry her. Fortunately, my brother-in-law ran in hot pursuit and caught her up before she actually reached the road. Picking her up he told her that he was going to take her into the house and give her a smack, explaining that the rules he had laid down were for her own safety and she had deliberately chosen not to obey them, putting herself in potential danger. It only took one little smack and the tearful child was sent upstairs to think about what she had done.

It wasn't long before she had calmed down and returned, apologising to dad. He explained to her again that she had to be punished as it was the only way she was going to learn, and even though at this young age she would not have understood it, he had to punish her because he loved her. (Great sermon illustration here.) My brother-in-law never had this sort of rebellion in his daughter from that day to this.

As all children are different some may not learn so quickly, and a parent has to be prepared to persevere. Discipline of this nature will need to be repeated until the child learns.

With my own children, I have never found that screaming at them has any positive effect, although like most parents it's an old habit that is very hard to break, especially if you are blessed with a very loud voice like mine. The worst punishment that I have ever needed to inflict on the boys as they grew older and were experimenting with how far they could push me, was a wallop with my slipper. That never needed to be hard as they were already in tears the minute I told them to bend over and touch their toes because they knew they had gone too far. I believe I only needed to use this extreme measure twice. I have never had to do this with our daughter; stern words have always been sufficient to get the message home to her.

I've discovered that so often a child's response to discipline depends on how much or little he loves and respects his parents. If the parents have not earned that love and respect, they will never be able to shout it or beat it into their child. The child will just get rapidly worse, suffering from rebellion, rejection, fear and hatred.

Here are just some of the prayers that children have written which will show children's workers some of the areas of hurt in children, and how they are going to need to pray for God's wisdom in dealing with them. As the family unit continues to disintegrate, and as divorce is escalating among Christian and non-Christian parents, tragically these 'horrors' are going to become more commonplace. Obviously I have left out the names of the children.

(1) We prayed that my dad would love me.

(2) Thank you, Lord, that I don't hate my dad any more.

(3) Thank you, Jesus, for freeing me from the hatred that was buried in my heart against my mother and my father.

(4) I was prayed for that God would take away my fear of getting divorced, because my mum has been twice.

(5) I prayed that I will have a love towards my stepfather, even though I find it difficult. And that the Lord will help me to be with him like I would my real father.

(6) I am not frightened of dying of leukaemia or heart problems now. I was frightened because my dad died of leukaemia.

(7) Dear God, I am not going to be afraid of car crashes and my mum and dad fighting.

(8) I was healed from hurt from when my dad left seven years ago.

(9) God has helped me to understand why my mum killed herself. She did it because she was depressed and she loved me.

(10) I am frightened because my dad might come and spoil our family 'cos Mum and Dad are not married.

(11) Lord, help me to stop crying over my mum and dad's divorce.

(12) Jesus, I am sorry that I ran out in front of a car and almost killed myself.

(13) I fear that my dad is going to get married to his girlfriend and care more about her children than me.

(14) Thank you, Lord, that I don't hate my brother any more, and please bring my family back together.

(15) Lord, I am not frightened of my mum any more, and I am not frightened of anything horrid on telly because I have faith in you and I know you're always there beside me.

(16) Dear Lord, please help my dad not to take it out on me and my brothers when he is cross, and help him not to smack us because I fear him very much.

(17) [Saying no to the voice of the evil one] I said no to hitting my sister when she was cuddling me. [From a little girl.]

(18) Tonight God made me sure that my daddy loves me even though he doesn't live with us, and I didn't think he did.

(19) Thank you so much. I came here feeling so depressed. I'm fifteen and I've just tried to commit suicide. I've been living by myself and I don't get on with my mum. My parents are divorced, but tonight when we prayed I physically felt my head and body

get lighter. I feel everything will now open up. I can now stop smoking and drinking.

(20) Dear Lord Jesus, I pray that my mum will come and see me more often because you know how much I miss her, and that she will come and see me and my sisters.

(21) I wanted to be prayed for because I do not like my brother, and also my dad has died and I had put that hatred on my brother.

(22) I had sex with my boyfriend. I am a Christian, he isn't. My conscience was pricked, but God is healing me. [From a very young girl.]

(23) A little voice said in my mind to laugh when mum and dad had a row and mum cried. But I said no to that voice.

7

Angels' Outing

(And now for a short intermission, and a short story.)

Part 1. The evening of the night before.

There are few events of more importance than that special day—sadly a very infrequent day—when Mum and Dad have put all the usual mundane Saturday chores to one side to devote the whole day to their family. The day has been looming up in the diary for months, but the closer it comes, the less they feel enthusiastic about it, as more and more so-called priorities seem to approach with it. For many, the pressure and guilt of having such a day proves too much for them and they end up having to inform their children that unfortunately it has been indefinitely cancelled. The disillusioned children are promised that they will have it another time, but the children, once let down, realise that there is more chance of getting Christmas presents in July.

Some parents, however, fight off all else and prove to be as good as their word, and our saga begins on the Friday night prior to the big day.

Where should they go and what should they do, is the big question under debate. Dad thinks they would enjoy a nice day fishing, because *he* would enjoy a nice day fishing, but Mum thinks that they would enjoy a nice day looking around the shops—of course, *she* would love a nice day looking around the shops—and with both these rather biased ideas in mind, Mum and Dad get into quite a heated debate together, each accusing the other of being selfish and trying to convince the other that the opposing suggestion is the last thing that the children would like to do.

A truce follows a short while later, and they decide to put their suggestions to the children and let *them* choose which one is the best plan for the day. The children sit listening intently as Mum and Dad communicate their ideas with all the skills of a loft insulation agent working on commission, trying to sell his wares to the owner of a flat-roofed house.

When their eloquent oratories finish, however, instead of the expected standing ovation, I'm afaid all they get is a polite raspberry from all the children in unison. Neither of those ideas are on their agendas for tomorrow.

Dad then thinks he has a brainwave. He tells the children to write down some of their ideas, then they can all decide together. After a very short time the children are standing in front of them, proudly holding up their sheets of paper which seem to have more suggestions on them than an opinion poll on what is wrong with the world today.

As each piece of paper is carefully scrutinised, opinions vary from staying at home and watching television all day, to going to Disneyland on Concorde. But the thing that Mum and Dad find most amazing is that with all these numerous suggestions, all the children have written down something different.

After thanking the children, the parents, now suffering from exhaustion, decide it is the children's bedtime, explaining that they need an early night so that they will be wide awake for the excitement that tomorrow will bring. As the shouts of 'But where are we going?' echo down the stairs, the confused adults shout back that it is going to be a surprise, but refrain from adding that it will also be a surprise for them as well.

With the children safely tucked in bed, fishing and shopping come back into the conversation.

Part 2. The night of the night before.

It was a restless night for Mum and Dad. They had laboriously read through all the 'What's On' columns in local papers, rung round to ask friends for suggesions, and even spent some time in prayer about it, but still were finding it hard to make a decision that everyone would be happy with. It proved to be a long night with little sleep, as two overactive adult minds refused to rest up, give up, and relax.

But, however long the night may have seemed, the morning came around far too soon.

Part 3. The big day is here

Weary and shattered, Mum and Dad have a rude awakening as their highly-keyed-up, excited children bounce all over their bed, with loud voices still screaming out the same question they had been asking when they climbed those stairs four thousand ideas ago. The good news is that Dad has an idea, but it would be suicide to reveal it in case it got the thumbs down. He just repeats that it will remain a surprise, and adds that they are going on a mystery tour. Now this is inspired thinking, as it has the advantage that if he suddenly feels like a change of guidance while driving, he can always take the car in another direction without having to confess to the family that he has changed his mind.

In a very short time breakfast is gulped down, and the car packed full with every conceivable useless item which hopefully will cover all needs whatever or wherever the destination turns out to be.

What could be better: the open road, the sun shining in the windows, and the children singing along to an Ishmael tape playing at full blast on the cassette machine. Everyone is blissfully happy.

More accurately, everyone is happy for the first five miles, and it is at this point that one of the children feels sick, and another needs the loo, and Dad is getting rather annoyed as Mum can't find where they are on the map. It is a bit premature, but they decide to pull in for a coffee break. After a short delay the wheels start rolling again and off they all go with the singing restarting. They are now even more determined that none of these little mishaps are going to be allowed to spoil their day.

Up until now, Dad has been tossing an imaginary coin in his mind for most of the journey as to whether he should drive to the seaside or the countryside. The seaside has just won by an imaginary head, and he overtakes a yacht on a trailer which is obviously heading in that direction. Cleverly, he still manages to keep a secret from the children, and inwardly he feels very pleased with himself when they arrive at Seatown and the children cheer as they get their first glimpse of the sea.

The seaside town is busy, and Dad is getting rather grumpy, both through not having enough sleep, and also through not having taken Mum's advice to park in the multi-storey car park. He is sure that he will find somewhere nearer to the beach, but his assurance has been unfounded, and he humbly returns to the multi-storey explaining how unusual it is that this extremely popular resort is so extremely popular.

But nobody minds; they load themselves up with every conceivable type of nautical apparatus and head for the golden sands.

Excitement has now taken over as they run all the way, with Mum and Dad as emotionally aroused as the children, but they come to a sudden halt when they see that Dad's idea of coming to the beach is not unique. Millions of other Dads have obviously had the same brainwave, and it is going to be like walking over a minefield, trying to avoid treading on some unsuspecting body.

Eventually, a few square feet of sand is located which they make their own territory by laying out a couple of blankets and quickly sitting on them. Then comes the great unveiling. The children tear off their clothes as fast as they can with no thought of modesty,

111

and on goes the swimming gear. Dad takes a little while longer to get his swimming trunks on, while Mum takes an age proving what a brilliant contortionist she is by putting on her bikini and still managing to keep her private parts from public viewing by using only one small towel.

Others lying around them are a little less discreet, which of course the children soon notice. The eldest one shouts out at the top of her voice: 'Mummy, why isn't that lady wearing a top?' Dad instinctively glances over, then, realising what he is peering at, quickly gets out a Christian magazine and starts to try and read it. Red with embarrassment, not instant sun tan, Mum notices that her child is pointing at a lady who has chosen to try for an almost-all-over, even tan. 'Shhh,' says Mum, 'just be quiet.' But she should have known that children will keep asking questions until they get an answer.

'Are you going to take your bra off too?' enquired the same voice who had obviously only very recently learned what a bra was, and now liked using the word. 'No, I am not,' said Mum. 'Christians don't do that sort of thing.' She hoped that the lady in question could not hear her, and that she wasn't a liberated Christian. 'Now just be quiet.'

'But Adam and Eve didn't wear any clothes,' continues the eager little theological student. 'Does that mean that they weren't Christians?' 'I'm going swimming,' says Mum, and she rushes off towards the sea.

By midday, they had swum, played cricket and football, made sandcastles and tunnels, and even found time to bury Dad in the sand. But now stomachs were informing them that it was lunch time.

Dad has still not learned his lesson from the night before, and he tries to decide democratically wha of food is the most desired. 'What does everyone like eating?' he asks, and one wants beans on toas one wants fish and chips, and the other really fancies a Chinese. Mum wants a salad. So up they all get, and to save any arguments Dad pops into the first place they come to, which happens to be a burger bar. He buys everyone a hamburger, which is the only thing they unanimously don't want.

Walking along the promenade they pass all the video game machines, and the children, relating the smell and the sound to that of a funfair, want to go in and see them. Dad and Mum say that they can, but tell them not to look at the machines, but more to look at the expressions on the faces of the people playing them. They are only in the hall a few minutes, and once out in the fresh air again one of the children asks why the people look so serious and sad when they are playing a game. Dad explains that like cigarettes, these machines can become addictive, which means that although it starts off as a bit of fun it often ends up that you can't stop playing them. They look sad because to some of them these machines have become such a major part of their lives, they have become like gods that they worship. Also, when they put their money into the machines, it is just like they are throwing their money away, which of course they could have spent on something that would have lasted or done them good.

Passing the bingo halls, they see similar expressions but from older folk.

Sensing that a bit of fun is needed, they find a crazy golf course. Having paid for their club and golf ball, off they go. Dad treats the game quite seriously and wants to prove to the children that he is a golfer that they can be proud of. Mum however sees it as a bit of fun, and just laughs as she pushes the ball nearer to the hole and kicks Dad's further away. The children just enjoy hitting the ball as hard as they can and watch people jump out of the way as it comes hurtling towards them.

Ice cream time follows and Dad has at last learned his lesson. Instead of asking what everyone wants, he just orders cornets all round, for which everyone is thankful and delighted.

After a return to the beach and another quick dip in the sea, which means a two-mile hike to find the water as it is now low tide, it is time to go home. The sun is going down and the car park ticket is expiring. The children are exhausted and fall asleep as soon as they get into the car.

As the handbrake is pulled on with a loud clicking noise outside their house, however, it is like an alarm bell. Everyone wakes up for tea, and ready for more fun in the evening.

Part 4. Good evening, Mums and Dads and boys and girls...

While everyone is munching their sandwiches, Dad is trying to think what they should do in the evening. He thinks of hiring a video film, but is a little bit disappointed that all the most exciting films seem to be full of profanities that he doesn't want to inflict on his children.

He is also concerned that many children's television programmes seem to be based on witchcraft, sorcery and the occult. Each week he goes through the television magazines and suggests to his children what they may enjoy watching. Then, after explaining why, he instructs them about programmes that would not be good for Christian children.

But tonight the telly can stay cold; it is games night. It starts with real old-fashioned family games like charades and other silly games, where no one actually wins and certainly no one loses. In fact most of the games end with everyone rolling about on the floor in uncontrollable fits of laughter.

Then, when the youngest goes to bed, out come the board games and attitudes become a little more serious. It is when they are about halfway through a game, right at the most exciting point, that the doorbell rings. Dad goes to the door and there is Mrs Dunnin. I failed to mention that both Mum and Dad run a home group and are responsible for the pastoral care of about a dozen folk, one of which happens to be Mrs Dunnin.

There are always genuinely needy folk that need help, but Mrs Dunnin is not one of them. She always had a long sad story to tell, always wants to be prayed for, and then always feels as bad, if not worse, after prayer than she did before. She is basically a lonely person who wants attention. Here on the doorstep Dad is faced with a problem; should he invite her in? The last thing he wants to be is inhospitable or rude, but would this spoil the day that he had specially set aside for his family, and, more to the point, would he ever finish his game?

Then he has an idea, 'Do come in, Mrs Dunnin,' he says, and he brings her into the room where the rest of the family are still sitting around the table looking at the games board.

The children get down from the table expecting to hear the words they have heard so often that they should go up to their rooms because Mum and Dad have to talk to someone. But no, this time it is different.

Dad explains to Mrs Dunnin that this is a special family day, and if she would like to sit in the chair, the family will pray over her—the children will start and then they will continue. Mrs Dunnin wasn't given the opportunity of going through her long spiel, and even though it was unusual for the children to pray for her, she agreed to Dad's suggestion. After a few minutes of prayer Mrs Dunnin is invited to join in the game, and it is then that the children see a different side to her; she is great fun and keeps making all sorts of jokes. Two hours later she leaves the house a much happier lady, not just because she has been welcomed as part of the family, but also because she has won the game.

At the end of the day the family thank God for each other, their health and wealth, and the fun that it is being part of his family. And do you know, the most amazing thing of all is that this is only Saturday and tomorrow is Sunday, which every dad and mum and boy and girl knows is still the best and most exciting day of the week.

8

Hand-Clapping, Foot-Stomping, Knee-Bowing Angels

It was always God's plan that children should be instruments of praise and worship.

Psalm 8:2 says, 'From the lips of children and infants you have ordained praise because of your enemies, to silence the foe and the avenger.' And Jesus himself quoted this scripture in Matthew 21 as in that triumphant, yet in some ways sad, procession he entered the Temple area and heard the children shouting, 'Hosanna to the Son of David.'

Children have a natural ability to praise and worship, but, as is so often the case, the enviroment and the influence of adults have encouraged the children to grow up in a way that tends to squeeze this heartfelt expression out of their little lives.

Praise and worship is a massive subject, and numerous books have been written on the meanings of these two well-used words. Most of these books, however, have tended to be for adults and used phrasing which few children can understand. It seems that most children are encouraged from a very early age to play a musical instrument, yet few are given instruction on how to develop as a musical instrument for the glory of God.

Having said this, however, the most important point we need to teach our children is that praise and worship is not just to do with music, nor is it just to do with Sundays and meetings. Praise and worship makes up how we live each day before God. The musical praise and worship gives us a chance to express outwardly the way we feel towards the Lord. This expression is not only natural for the believer, it is also vital to him. That is why I feel it is worth taking a chapter to look at it in some detail.

For young children, simple and clear definition is important, and I would instruct them that praise is giving thanks, while worship is adoration. Let us look at these in more detail.

One of my favourite scriptures is 1 Thessalonians 5:16–22. This sums up so much of my teaching to children: 'Be joyful always; pray continually; give thanks in all circumstances, for this is God's will for you in Christ Jesus. Do not put out the Spirit's fire; do not treat prophecies with contempt. Test everything. Hold on to the good. Avoid every kind of evil.'

When someone comes and says to you that they are not sure what God's will for them is, quote them that scripture, emphasising: 'Give thanks in all circumstances, for this is God's will for you in Christ Jesus.' Often when people are needing guidance and answers, once they begin thanking God, their guidance and answers seem to come so much clearer and more quickly.

This whole chapter could be filled with scriptures that instruct us to give thanks to God, proving what a very important part of our Christian life God would like this to be.

Sometimes giving thanks to God is hard for Christian children because they have been brought up in this modern generation to believe that the world owes them, and that they deserve all they are given. Through being spoilt, they have not learned the importance of saying thank you and being thankful to others.

When children are not taught to give thanks for what they receive, it has a far more harmful effect than just making them rude and impolite to those around them. It also teaches them to be disrespectful and irreverent to God. These children will need to be re-educated before they will be capable of entering into real praise.

Out of the thousands of adults and children I have spent time ministering to, less than ten per cent would come up and show any gratitude, even though I know that they have enjoyed what I have done. Please don't get me wrong. It's not important that we are for ever being patted on the back, but an indication of how much we really appreciate God can be found by how much we really appreciate the members of his body. It is important that we learn to show our appreciation, and that isn't just by giving somebody a round of applause.

I remember after one Praise Party two people approached me; one was a tiny little girl who thanked me and told me how much she had enjoyed the evening, and the other was a treasurer, who said nothing but just thrust an envelope in my hand without even a smile. I received more of a blessing from that little girl than however many digits were written on that cheque; I guess it's got something to do with being a cheerful giver.

Although true thanks comes from our hearts, we usually express it by action. Sometimes we pat each other on the back; other times we may embrace or kiss as a sign of our appreciation. At events, if we have enjoyed being entertained, we may clap, shout, whistle or even stand to our feet to let those who have given to us know that we are thankful.

The Bible also talks about many ways in which people, through movement, gave thanks to God. Here are some in alphabetical order:

Bowing

'Therefore God exalted him [Jesus] to the highest place and gave him the name that is above every name, that at the name of Jesus every knee should bow, in heaven and on earth and under the earth, and every tongue confess that Jesus Christ is Lord, to the glory of God the Father' (Philippians 2:9–10).

Bowing and lying flat on the ground

'Then David said to the whole assembly, "Praise the Lord your God." So they all praised the Lord, the God of their fathers; they bowed low and fell prostrate before the Lord and the King' (1 Chronicles 29:20).

Clapping and shouting

'Clap your hands, all you nations; shout to God with cries of joy' (Psalm 47:1).

Dancing and music

'Let them praise his name with dancing and make music to him with tambourine and harp' (Psalm 149:3).

Hands raised high

'Ezra praised the Lord, the great God; and all the people lifted their hands and responded, "Amen! Amen!"' (Nehemiah 8:6).

High-energy dancing

'David, wearing a linen [cloth] danced before the Lord with all his might' (2 Samuel 6:14).

Jumping

'He jumped to his feet and began to walk. Then he went with them into the temple courts, walking and jumping, and praising God' (Acts 3:8).

Standing up

'And the Levites...said, "Stand up and praise the Lord your God, who is from everlasting to everlasting"' (Nehemiah 9:5).

These are just a few of the many ways in which people praised God in the Bible, and each one of these had more variations than one could imagine.

My observation of children is that for years they have been suppressed and not taught about the many ways of releasing their praise. Some have learned that praise is just singing a hymn, and think that all that is required for them to express their thanks to God is to stand politely until the countless verses have been sung and then to sit down again. Others have been taught that their praise must be expressed with reverence, which they think is being still and remaining silent, and many churches are actually proud to have installed horrible long hard wooden benches called pews which, like the stocks of old, make sure that nobody can move, even if they want to. Some could be very courageous and dance on top of them, but then they would probably be thrown out for vandalism.

Of course there is a place for stillness and silence, but don't confuse children into thinking that these are the definition of reverence, or else you are in danger of writing off most of God's friends in the Bible. Reverence is shown in our feelings towards God and not necessarily in the way we humbly and honestly express them.

Little children are naturally bouncy and energetic, and when they do something they tend to do it like King David did, with all their might. I wonder, if we invited David to come to one of our meetings, how many of us would let him preach but never allow him to lead the praise and worship. Some people have told me that I am extreme, but compared with David I think I'm a shy, reserved introvert. I do care what people think of me, but David didn't. All he seemed to care about was pleasing his best friend and that was God whom he loved and obeyed.

One of my aims has been to restore children's natural expressions to them so they don't have to fit into the reserved and restricted adult mould that we have chosen to bury ourselves in.

I remember going to one fellowship in the Midlands, and while praying about what praise songs to sing I felt that I should do a song which I didn't particularly like. The song encourages people to clap and dance as part of their praise to Father God. As the meeting began I noticed all the children had come down to the front to get a good view. I started singing this well-worn song and both children and adults alike just watched me in amazement, standing as still as cement statues with their eyes popping out in unbelief, as I sang and danced to it.

Before you ask, yes, I was totally embarrassed. I had come to encourage them in praise and worship, not do a one-man Come Dancing exhibition at the front. Determined not to give up, however, I played it a couple more times and on about the third run through I noticed that some of the children had started tapping their feet. Well, this was a one hundred per cent improvement, so I thought I would sing this song— which was rapidly getting more boring and repetitive to me—a few more times.

By the fifth time all the children were dancing and singing, and the adults' feet had started tapping. Some had even started to smile. Always being willing to push a point to extremes, I continued to play this chorus and it must have been about the tenth time through that everyone began to dance and sing and praise God. In fact, I think I was the only one who had stopped due to wearing myself out on the nine previous renditions.

No, I do not do this at every meeting, but it was right to do it at this one because through it I learned a few important lessons.

The first was that it was the children who were used to release the adults. It was only as the older folk saw these young ones enjoying praising God that they decided to join in with them.

The other important thing that happened was, as everyone joined in together, a heaviness lifted off the meeting. People became more at ease and relaxed, and as I preached a little later in the meeting I noticed that because they were more relaxed they were so much more willing to respond as God spoke to them on personal needs and issues.

Children enjoying their praise and worship are not only a blessing to the rest of the church, but also an example of how free we older children can be before our heavenly Father.

I invariably meet children's leaders who treat me as some sort of 'pied piper'. When I take a meeting, their children respond, but when they take a similar sort of meeting they seem to get nowhere.

I have no magical or sinister powers, but I do believe that children and adults are led by example. I would never teach people to do things that I would not be willing to do myself, and I would not sing praise songs which encourage folks to raise their hands or dance unless I was willing to do it. In fact, I have gone as far as to tell people not to sing certain lines of songs that require certain movements if they won't do them. It is ridiculous to sing words that we don't mean.

Leading by example is important for nearly every area of the Christian life. There is the argument, of course, that the children just imitate and don't understand what they are doing. For many of the very young ones this is a valid point, but I think of what Paul said in 1 Corinthians 4:16: 'Therefore I urge you to imitate me.' To copy what is good and biblical, whatever the motives (or lack of motives in this case), is not such a bad thing. Subconsciously, we all imitate others.

I have observed that if the child is taught well, it is not long before he has stopped copying and is expressing praise of his own volition and being very sincere in his actions.

Another thing I have noticed with children is that their praise has very little to do with their personalities and temperaments. They, like us, would just use these as an excuse for not being as free as God would like them to be.

A Christian musical called Come Together was very popular some years ago, and this was quite revolutionary as it taught people to clap and raise their hands. The only problem was that many in the audiences were not in the Spirit, and it taught people how to be extrovert rather than how to be free in the Spirit.

God does not want us all to be extrovert of character, but he does want us to be so full of that Holy Spirit boldness that we are not frightened to do anything that pleases God.

The extrovert who is not sensitive to the Spirit of God can be a worship leader's nightmare in a meeting. I have had them in my meetings, and while the loud praise is being expressed they are fine, but as the mood of the meeting changes and the music quietens down and becomes very gentle, sadly our extrovert praiser fails to recognise this and still leaps around bashing his tambourine like a maniac.

God has made children with different personalities; how boring the world would be if they were all the same. The last thing I would ever want to do is put them in an Ishmael mould so that they all came out as little replicas of me. But I do want to teach them to lose their inhibitions and learn what it is like to be free in their praise and worship.

Let us go on from praise, and now look at worship.

We must get out of our heads the idea that praise is the fast songs and worship is the slow ones. As I mentioned in my definition earlier of thanksgiving and adoration, these words are much vaster than just being associated with songs and their speed or rhythm.

Children so often need a picture to help them understand.

One of the Greek words for worship is proskun. The meaning of this word is simply 'to kiss the hand', and it is used over fifty times in the New Testament.

To give children a picture of this I wrote a song called, 'I'll kiss the hand of Jesus', which went like this:

> I'll kiss the hand of Jesus, yes I will.
> I'll kiss the hand of Jesus, yes I will.
> As I see the hole where the nail has been,
> I realise it was my sin,
> That marred those beautiful hands,
> That scarred those beautiful hands.
>
> The hand that held the little ones sitting on his knee,
> The hand that only taught to love and care,
> The hand that rescued Peter from drowning in
>   the sea,
> Was soon to feel the cross that it would bear.

126

The hand that was tied up for the love that it had
   shown,
The hand that didn't resist the enemy,
The hand that didn't scream as the blunt pins
   held it high,
The fingers reaching out to victory.

The hand that couldn't die now writes the Book
   of Life,
This hand also shares the bread and wine,
And Jesus says 'Christian, if you want to worship me,
Just come and kiss this hand of mine.'

This song helps children use their imagination to
understand why we adore our Lord, and just a little bit
of what heartfelt worship really is.

I firmly believe that children need to know the significance of the suffering and pain of the Lord Jesus
upon the cross if they are to really know worship.

At one meeting, I spent quite a few minutes explaining this to about 400 eight- to eleven-year-olds. They
were so quiet you could have heard a pin drop. After
this I sang a song of worship, and without giving the
children instruction as to how to express their worship, I told them to tell the Lord how much they loved
him.

It was at this point that we all felt the power of God
in a very special way, and many of the children spon-
taniously fell on their knees worshipping the Lord.
Some started crying out to God, while others were
weeping before him as they considered the cost of
Calvary. I have yet to be in a meeting with adults

where there has been such a deep, sincere level of Christ-centred worship. There is no doubt about it, these little ones really know how to praise and worship.

As I close this chapter it may be worth sharing a few thoughts on songwriting. Songs are much easier to write than most people imagine, and I would encourage any children's workers, even if they are only slightly musical, to try writing them.

Before you start composing praise and worship, have a go at writing a Scripture song; they are the simplest. All you need to do is find a short verse of Scripture and put a melody to it. It does not have to rhyme, but it does need to be easy to sing. This of course has a dual purpose as it not only teaches the children a new song, but also teaches them Scripture. At this stage involve some of your other leaders who may not be musicians to think up some actions or dances if and when the words are appropriate.

Praise and worship songs do require a little more thought. A writer needs to consider what age group the song is primarily for, what he wants to convey through his words and music, and what he hopes it will achieve for those singing it.

The first praise and worship song that people write usually sounds like the following:

> Jesus died for me.
> He died at Calvary.
> How happy I should be.
> Now from sin I am set free.

A good start—factual, accurate, simple, and I'm sure easy to sing. The more you write, however, the more creative and expressive and less clichéd and predictable your songs will become. After a short while your song will say a similar thing but in a different way, and may sound something like:

> Lord Jesus, I'm so thankful that you gave your life for me,
> For the pain and suffering endured upon that cross at Calvary.
> The more I think about it, the more happy I should be,
> 'Cause from the sin that once ensnared me,
> I've been released and am set free.

There are one or two words which small children may not understand, but I am a keen believer in stretching their vocabulary as well as their spiritual lives. Rather than use one-syllable words all the time, use longer ones and explain to the children what they mean.

As you progress in songwriting you will want to get away from the obvious rhyming patterns and also the 'da de da de da de da' stanzas, and you may end up changing your song to:

> I'm so thankful that you gave Your life, Lord Jesus,
> And it's you I want to worship, it's you whom I adore.
> You've filled my life with happiness, since your blood has set me free,
> And the sin that once ruled in my life, will not rule me any more.

And so you keep working on it until you feel it says what you want to the age group you want say it to. By the way, as you may have guessed, I have not spent days composing these three stages of a worship song. It has taken me, hold on, I'll just look at my watch, yes, about ten minutes, and that includes the time it's taken to type it out on the computer, answer a phone call, and drink my coffee. So you can see how easy it is; you've got no excuse. There is a great need for new praise songs which children can enjoy. If we want to keep our children in line with the Bible's advice to sing a new song, we will have to write songs first.

Remember, children love songs with instructions of how to praise and worship.

I've included the following lines from songs I have written, which always get the children participating.

> Lord you put a tongue in my mouth and I want to
>   sing to you.
> Lord you put some feet on my legs and I want to
>   dance to you.
> Lord you put some hands on my arms which I want
>   to raise to you.
> I will wave my hands in praise and adoration.
> So we're marching along, singing a song.
> He's got the victory so let's really shout.
> So we're raising up our banner stating Jesus is
>   victorious.
> Some of us whisper the praise we bring.

Finally, in our meetings we want there to be a time when the children can forget about the actions, not think about dance, not worry about the music, even ignore people around them, and just think about the Lord.

> I'm looking up to Jesus.
> His face is shining beauty.

I'm feeling so unworthy,
Yet his Spirit leads me on.
I'm looking up to Jesus.
His radiance surrounds me.
I feel so pure and clean.
A taste of heaven on earth.

I'm looking up to Jesus.

9

Old Saints Versus Young Angels?

I wonder what happened to the family service, the time when all ages of the family could meet together to worship, learn, and also to enjoy each other's company. And I wonder if there ever really was such an event. Most of what passes as a family service today is not worth pursuing and has the smell of total disaster about it.

The church has been as guilty as secular society of encouraging families to split up, and we have been eager to promote the age and generation gap.

As I mentioned when talking about Sunday schools, Jesus didn't divide the children from the parents, or the babies from their mother's arms. There were no 18-certificate ratings on his meetings; they were for all the family.

Just imagine, if that huge five thousand plus crowd had consisted only of adults they would have all starved, for it was a young lad who was the possessor of the five small loaves and the two fish.

Children and adults need to meet regularly together. Children will learn a lot by watching adults, and as I continually try to prove, adults can also learn a lot by watching children. Let me give you some reasons.

The children need to have a chance to contribute to the whole congregation, whether their gifting is musical, preaching or pastoring. They will learn more by being allowed not only to observe 'the experts' and how they do it, but also to work alongside them and be taught practically. The best football teams are the ones that have a youth training programme, which not only teaches the youth theory and how to play against other lads of their own age, but also gives them a chance to play against the first team and see the skills and the standard that will be required of them in the years to come.

I wonder how many leaders realise that ninety per cent of all the future ministries that will be needed in their fellowship are already in their children's meetings. If they don't give the children the opportunity to blossom and develop, they will put all their talents into careers, business and making money, which in time will take their minds and hearts off God. Contrary to popular belief, imported adult ministries are not necessarily God's ideal and not necessarily the best.

I also believe that we need to be an example to a world which, on the whole, has lost its way in being able to communicate and befriend others outside its age and generation. Children and parents so often have little communication between them, and teens and parents have even less.

Children are quite rightly encouraged not to talk to older people on the streets, because we live in a perverted age when people are roaming our streets with the sole intention of kidnapping our children and using them to satisfy their own evil lusts and desires. Not a day seems to pass without us reading or hearing about some maniac who has destroyed a young life.

In other places, however, we have the other extreme where many older folks live in fear and cannot go out of their homes because gangs of children are waiting to mug and rob them. I'll never forget the time I was in Manchester doing a mission, and as I went for a walk outside I saw an uncontrollable mob of young boys and girls walking down the street destroying anything that got in their path. Later that evening, while we were praying in one room of the building, they crept in and stole the whole public address system, part of which happened to be screwed to the walls.

When I was in South Wales doing some street evangelism, I met some tiny children who, for the whole time that I was singing and talking, just stood there shouting the most obscene swear words that I had ever heard.

Tragically the age gap in church life is following society's trend. The children, through what they have read, heard or been taught, fear and have little respect for older folk, while the older folk feel exactly the same way about the children. How many Christian meetings have you been to where the young and the old trust each other and enjoy each other's company? I'm afraid that at the majority of meetings I have been to, people either stayed with their own age group or spent time with those they already knew quite well. They certainly did not go out of their way to make new relationships.

It's common sense that to keep the adults in one room and the children in another is not going to help this problem; far from it, it is just going to widen the gap even further. We must have regular times when all ages of God's family can be together, so that they cannot only be taught how to communicate with each other, but also shown how to love, honour, trust and respect each other.

But is bringing all the ages together regularly going to help? After all, most congregations do this either for a short time each Sunday morning or maybe for a whole meeting once a month, and the truth is that very little has changed. The simple answer is 'no'. We have tried these meetings, and these are ones that we have entitled 'family service', but very rarely are they suitable for the whole family. Usually they are just a normal adult service with a talk and maybe one song thrown in for the children.

If we want to have a real family service, we must be willing to alter our traditions and change the whole meeting around so that it is enjoyable to the boys and girls as well as the adults.

I want the children to look forward to Sunday as the best day of the week. I want them to be more excited about going to worship than they would be about going to school, or even to some social or recreational activity. I would also like to see them pleased by the prospect of meeting up with friends who are not just the same age and from the same school.

But are we willing to make the necessary changes, and are we even able to? Let me talk through some of the changes I've discovered that have been helpful. Please remember that very few people find change easy, and it will mean a lot of give and take and patience from the older folk, who should, of course, be the more mature.

Let's start right at the beginning on how things tend to be, but not necessarily how they should be. Here is a little over-dramatised fictitious story about a family, a Sunday morning, and a typical monthly family service.

The Crumbles

The Crumble family are having breakfast. Well, when I say the family, that does not include Jimmy because he, despite the numerous shouts of, 'This is the last time I am going to tell you,' from his mum, is still reading comics in bed. Talking about Mum, she, as usual, is trying to do 101 things at once. In one hand she has the potato peeler preparing the Sunday lunch, in the other hand is the hair dryer drying her hair, and her mouth is full of cornflakes. It's true that a woman's work is never done, especially on a Sunday. I wonder if she can be thankful that this is her day of rest.

Now Dad on the other hand spent five minutes at the breakfast table, but unfortunately his half-drunk cup of coffee has turned tepid and is rapidly congealing due to the fact that he has been on the phone for the last ten minutes to Mrs Bloggins. She only rang up to ask for a lift to the meeting, but she has ended up relaying to him her life history for the umpteenth time.

Darren and baby Sarah are, however, at the table, but Darren has just accidentally tipped the cornflakes all over the floor in an effort to find the free plastic sword and sorcery model of the hideous hulk from hell, while Sarah is discovering just how far a spoonful of rusk will travel when flicked in a certain way with her spoon.

Amid all the reigning chaos, they are trying to prepare themselves for the Sunday morning meeting which is due to begin in half an hour.

Today is a very special day as they have decided to try a new church meeting they have seen advertised; a monthly 'family worship' service where all ages are welcomed. It's not that they don't like their own service and want to be disloyal; it is just that they feel it important to spend time worshipping God together as a family, but their leaders don't seem to agree with them. Anyway, that is not the burning question; the burning question is, will they be ready in time?

The answer to that is, yes, albeit with much wailing and gnashing of teeth. Our intrepid family does manage to get to the building on time—well, ten minutes late actually—but unbeknown to them everyone comes late due to the fact that the leaders' watches are obviously always ten minutes slow and they always start late.

On the doorstep are two very large men whose mammoth-sized grins a Cheshire cat would covet. They are not minders, armed guards, sentries or bouncers; no, they are the welcoming committee.

Now, as to which member of the family they welcome first depends on whether the husband or wife is the obvious leader of the family. If in doubt they have made it a rule to go for the larger of the two. The only time this rule may get broken is if the lady is extremely attractive; then she would automatically get the priority.

Different doormen have different welcoming customs: some shake hands, some embrace, and some even kiss, but they would only give their brotherly kiss to the sisters.

These men, though, discover Mr Crumble first and shake him firmly by the hand, booming out in loud voices those somewhat worn out words: 'Welcome, brother.' This means, of course, that the doormen don't know the Crumbles family name, and are too embarrassed to ask what it is in case they have been before and they have forgotten it.

Then Mrs Crumble gets a similar welcome. The warm welcomers have been unaware of the presence of any children until one of them falls over baby Sarah's pushchair and the other treads on Jimmy's foot.

'Oh,' they exclaim, their smiles rapidly fading, 'we see you've brought the children with you. How nice.' Then, in true Crufts style, they go round and pat all three children on the head.

On a normal Sunday they would have taken Jimmy and Darren down a dark little corridor leading to the store room-cum-Sunday school where they would not be seen and hopefully not heard either. But this morning it is the 'family service' and they have to allow them into the adult's enclosure.

The doormen remind the children that they are about to enter the house of God, so they must be opposite to everything that God made them to be: that is, they must keep silent, sit still, and show no external signs of happiness or else they will be dumped back in the Sunday school cells where children really belong.

Baby Sarah, though, is still banned. She is still too young to be considered a member of the family of God, and anyway, a lot of money has been spent to sound-proof a room at the back of the building especially for her age group. A large sort of fish tank window has been installed so that all the parents are able to see their children crying without hearing them, and all the tinies are able to see their parents paying no attention to their screams and tears.

Once Sarah is out of the way behind closed doors, left in the capable hands of a retired spinster affectionately named Auntie Helga, plus a few teenagers who want to skive the meeting, the rest of the family creep into the cold building and find a spare hard wooden bench. Here they sit quietly waiting for the leaders to enter from the closed door on the right hand side of the platform.

All is quiet; you could hear a pin drop. The silence is only broken by occasional tuts that echo around the room as the odd mother tries in vain to smuggle an infant in, or one of the children present drops a pencil or whispers to his mum that he wants to go to the toilet.

Eventually the leaders arrive, and apart from the initial welcome which includes a special hello to all the children present, it is hard to work out how this is any different from a normal adult service.

'Let us all begin by worshipping the Lord together.' This is hard for the Crumbles to do, bearing in mind the events of the morning so far. Dad is wondering if he has locked the front door of the house; then, when he convinces himself that he has, he starts wondering if he has locked up his car. Mum, meanwhile, is wondering if she has turned the oven on, and hopes that baby Sarah is not being too much of a nuisance. The boys are not so much worried about how the meeting is going to start; it is more important for them to know when it is going to end. For any of the family to switch straight onto worship is an impossibility.

The first song is a favourite, but it contains the word 'resplendent'. As Darren tugs his dad's jacket and asks him what it means he is met with a severe, 'Be quiet, Darren. Now is not the time to be asking questions like that. I will tell you when we get home.' What his dad really means is that he doesn't have a clue either, but when he gets home he will look it up in the dictionary.

As well as difficult words, the children are also faced with difficult tunes, and some of the songs even sound to them like they don't have any tune at all. Darren thinks this is another point worth bringing up, so he turns to his mum this time and asks her why the song has no tune. She replies that the tune is not important, and he should just concentrate on the words.

After some prayers that seem longer than Samson's hit list, and the reading of what seems like Psalm 119 from the Amplified Bible, everyone sits down with anticipation as the children's spot is about to happen.

'And now,' says the leader, 'a special song for the children.' This is the most predictable part of the service. Everyone except the Crumbles knows that if hymn books are being used they will sing 'All Things Bright and Beautiful', and if they are not it will either be, 'The Wise Man Built his House Upon The Rock' or 'Deep and Wide'. This is the one and only silly time in the meeting when people can be themselves, act like idiots and join in with the actions. The songs are introduced as 'oldies but goldies', but Jimmy, having sung them every week in his own Sunday school since he started, thinks that they would be better named, 'oldies and mouldies'.

It is during this song that many of the older folk start to relax as they watch the children enjoying themselves. Some of them even start making funny noises like 'Ahhh' and the odd one or two even manage a faint smile. But all too soon for the oldies, and not soon enough for some of the children, the song has finished, and the courageous few that adventurously stood up to do the actions are now told to sit down again.

A blackboard easel is ceremoniously carried onto the platform and a large board with green felt is placed on it. The preacher then comes forward to give a special talk to the children. He has decided on Zaccheus as his subject as he feels it is easy for the children to understand, and anyway the local Bible bookshop only had this story left in their flannelgraph section. Apart from Darren whispering that they heard this story the week before in their own Sunday school, old and young sit back waiting for the show to begin.

Sadly, a good adult preacher is not always a good communicator with children, as this preacher proves. As well as using long words, he has a boring voice and little personality. He does have a good sense of humour though, but again it is an adult sense of humour, and while the adults are, metaphorically speaking, rolling in the aisles, the children just look bewildered and wonder what is so funny. The only thing that appeals to Darren and Jimmy's sense of humour and gives them the giggles is when the bits of felt keep falling off the preacher's board and go floating down to the floor, but Mum tells them to be quiet and listen to what is being said.

Being a good preacher, he sums up with three points at the end. Unfortunately he lost the children's attention a long time ago, so the points tend to fall on stony ground, as by now have most of his felt figures.

A short prayer for the children is the signal that the meeting has now finished for them. It may as well be the benediction. Out come the *Beano* and *Dandy* annuals, Postman Pat, and the special offer mammoth colouring and activity books. The children know that they have at least an hour to kill and the sensible ones have come well prepared.

There is, of course, nothing wrong with what follows: more long songs, more long prayers, another extra-long preach, followed by more long prayers and a final long song. If a survey is held for the adults on what they think of the meeting, the honest ones will say that everything could have been a lot shorter. Those not so honest, however, will put any flaw down to the children being present.

As the meeting concludes, the Crumble family pick up little Sarah from the collection point of the crèche. She is in a terrible state, having cried for Mum for the last hour, and even Auntie Helga's seemingly endless supply of sweets has not taken her mind off the fact that she wanted her mum.

On the way home the two boys are irritable and start fighting. They have sat quietly for so long that they are desperate to let off steam. Dad tells them to behave themselves and reminds them where they have just been and what a good meeting they have just had. 'I thought it was boring and I don't want to go back there again,' Darren and Jimmy say together, with such good timing that it sounds like it has been rehearsed.

Both Dad and Mum decide not to talk to the children about the family service any more; after all, it was a privilege for the children to be invited into the adults' meeting and they convince themselves that deep down it was doing their children a lot of good. For the children's sake they also decide it will be good to go back each month, and whenever Jimmy or Darren moan, 'On no, we're not going to that boring meeting with all those old fogies, are we?', their reply is, 'Don't complain, it's wonderful that we can go and worship the Lord as a family.'

Oh, and as for baby Sarah, she does eventually get used to Auntie Helga, but as she gets older she also needs ministry for rejection. Here endeth the story.

A typical family and a typical service? I hope not. Wildly exaggerated? I hope so. Let me close by giving a bit of positive advice.

Our fellowship has run family services every Sunday morning for sixteen years, and I have personally been involved in leading hundreds if not thousands of 'all-age celebrations'.

True, it is not easy to satisfy all ages, but I would also repeat what I said at the beginning of this chapter: regular real family meetings are essential for today's church. Let me give you some hints that I have discovered over the years to be the keys for success.

(1) Prepare for the seven-to-eight-year-olds. Those under eight will be able to understand most of what you do, and those over eight will not only understand it, but in time thoroughly enjoy it.

(2) Encourage parents to sit with their children wherever possible and 'adopt' any leftovers. This makes it easier for the parents to be in easy reach of

their own children and vice versa. The meeting itself will not just be centred around blood families; everything that is done will be for everyone to participate in together as this is a meeting for the broader family of God.

(3) Unless the Spirit of God does something very special, aim for the meeting to last one to one-and-a-half hours long. If the leader keeps his eye on the children he will soon see when it has gone on too long.

(4) If any babies get the shrieks, teach Mum or Dad to nip outside the door for a few minutes until the child has quietened down. In an emergency the occasional biscuit or sweet works wonders, although this is only for extreme cases. I would tend not to encourage it, because the child can cotton on to the fact that every time he shrieks in a meeting he gets a biscuit. It doesn't take long for babies to learn when they can make a din and when they need to be quiet.

(5) This is not designed to be a Bible study and you will not have the time for great exegesis, but we all know that there are plenty of other nights in the week for that. Nearly all churches or fellowships have mid-week meetings specifically for deeper study for the adults. Sunday is supposed to be the family day.

(6) The offering. If it is to be evangelistic, it is best to leave a box at the door which both your regular adults and children will soon get used to finding. If, however, you choose to take up an offering, take it near the beginning of the meeting. Otherwise the children's money will end up rolling all over the floor, just when you don't want it to.

(7) Toys. You will need to teach your parents that certain noisy toys are not suitable for tinies in a family service. Remember that what to you may seem com-

mon sense, to others is far from common and even further from sense. Define everything clearly, it saves a lot of trouble.

(8) Toilets. Do make sure that the children have been to the toilet before you all settle down, then you will know that they can last for at least the next hour, if not longer, and you won't be trundling in and out of the door all the time with them. With small children and toilet training I understand this is difficult, but it is sometimes more thoughtful to the other people in the meeting if your child can wear soft-soled or quiet shoes so that going in and out does not become a major distraction to the whole meeting.

(9) Discipline. Amid all the fun and noise the family service is not a mad house. It is a time for us to worship Almighty God together. Parents need to be taught to correct their children, and no child should be left running wildly around the hall, especially not at the front. There is nothing worse, or more of a distraction, when you are trying to sing or speak through the microphone if little Jenny is swinging from the stand, with her parents oblivious to or even smiling at your plight. This one requires a lot of patience; it will take the parents as long to learn their role and responsibility as it will their child.

I guarantee that in the long term all these hints are worth working at.

Here is an order of service that starts at 10.30 am:

10.15: Everything set up; musicians playing some nice lively music as people enter. No singing; you want people to be welcoming each other.

10.30: Always start on time. A welcome given from the front, and a run down of the order of service for any visitors present so that they know roughly what is going to happen. Prayer.

10:35: Scripture songs that are very lightweight, mainly to allow folk to settle down, relax and feel at home.

10:45: Once relaxed, start off with plenty of noise, using songs of praise which involve movement. Give the opportunity for dance and expression, but never force it so that visitors feel threatened. Watch those children go!

10:55: Quieten everything down; sing gentle songs which simply tell the Lord how much you love him. At this stage the children may start to turn off, so you could make a point of teaching them how they need to be involved in worship. During this time there may be open prayer, plus spiritual gifts being exercised, and if unusual things happen explain to the children what God is doing.

11:15: Ask all the children to sit on the floor in front of you because now is the time for their talk. Choose a Bible story, such as Joseph and his amazing coat, and either tell the story with pictures (on card or overhead projector) or get some of your talented drama people to act it out. You can have fun with this, and the children always remember something visual. Have one main point at the end of the story for the children to remember.

11:25: Follow the story with two special action choruses for the tinies.

11:30: Children are given an activity sheet which is related to the story, and they go back to their seats to do it. This may contain a word search, a puzzle, and certainly plenty of things to colour in. Remember, you will need a supply of coloured pencils to hand out to

147

visitors along with the sheets. Your own children should bring their own pencils.

11:30: A ten-minute application of Joseph for the adults. Although this sounds very short, you must bear in mind that they have already had the basic story, so you needn't go over that again. It's surprising how much content you can get into ten minutes; it's cutting out the waffling that is the hard thing for most preachers. Remember, it will take more preparation than if you had two hours to preach.

11:40: An appeal may be needed, or a short time of ministry arising from the sermon. If you bring people out to the front to pray for them, ask any children if they want to come and join you. Let them pray if they want to, or otherwise just let them listen to you so they can learn how to pray.

11:50: Finish with praise, worship, marching around the hall, prayer, or whatever seems appropriate. And encourage the children to show their completed masterpieces to the person who did the children's talk. Maybe next week a gallery can be made of them on one of the walls so that the less fortunate older ones who were not allowed to have an activity sheet can see what they got up to.

Finally, don't be frightened to ask the children what they thought of the meeting. Like adults, there will always be those with a few grumbles, but wouldn't it be music to your ears to hear a child say that they thoroughly enjoyed the family service...and they can't wait until the next one!

10

Angels' Delight?

I remember going to Sunday school. It was not a million miles away from the description I gave in the previous chapter of the Crumbles' story. While the second hymn was being sung we would all file out down a corridor until we eventually arrived in a shabby little room, illuminated if we were lucky by a couple of ten-watt light bulbs.

It was always a job to squeeze us all in, and that was not because the room was too small—it was quite a good size room. It was more due to the fact that we had to share this room with old projectors and screens, blackboard easels that must have been purchased during the war, toys that a playgroup would use on week-day mornings, the minister's old waders that had been used for the odd baptismal service, and lots of other odd bits of old rubbish. It could be politely summed up by saying that we were in the church's junk room.

Our singing would be accompanied by an out-of-tune piano, and if we were not singing 'Deep and Wide' or 'The Wise Man Built his House Upon the Rock', we were forced to choose any of our favourite songs from a tattered CSSM chorus book that we held in our hands. The trouble was that we had no favourites; in fact we didn't like any of them, except 'Deep and Wide' and 'The Wise Man Built his House Upon the Rock', of course.

After making noises which some would call singing, we went through an exercise called 'sword drill'. This was really just a race to see who was the first person to find a verse in the Bible without tearing out too many pages. Once the verse had been found the competition continued by seeing who could get the most laughs out of making the long Old Testament names sound silly and funny.

When enough Bibles had been demolished, or we were out of control with laughter, we would sit down, and depending on our age and not our ability, we would either hear another exciting adventure from *Jungle Doctor*, or watch a flannelgraph and count the bits as they fell on the floor. Failing this we'd get a long boring sermon from someone who had been relegated from the main church service to the ladies meeting because the church had found him boring, then further relegated from the ladies meeting to us because even they found him too boring.

I remember the teachers. I think many would have prefered to have been anywhere except with us. They only ended up in this position because there was no other function they could do in the church, or else they were the teenagers who took the job because it was the lesser of two evils, the greater being having to sit through the morning service.

Have you ever wondered why we children continued going? Well, it was for two reasons: firstly, because our parents made us, and secondly, because we wanted to fill up our sticker books and get our free Bible at the end of the year. The sticker collecting was not so much an incentive to us; it was more like a beginner's course in the art of deceit and gambling. If we were cunning we could still miss a morning, still get a sticker, and still get something for nothing at the end of the year.

Maybe I was the odd one out, but I didn't like proper school from Monday to Friday anyway, even though it was run by trained professionals, so having to face another school on Sundays run by non-enthusiastic amateurs was pretty grim to put it mildly.

Religious education for children has been around for longer than most encyclopaedias can remember. In fact, right from the beginning of time children were taught by parents and others about the Lord God.

Psalm 78 says,

> O my people, hear my teachings; listen to the words of my mouth. I will open my mouth in parables, I will utter things hidden from of old—things we have heard and known, things our fathers have told us. We will not hide them from our children; we will tell the next generation the praiseworthy deeds of the Lord, his power and the wonders he has done. He decreed

statutes for Jacob and established the law in Israel, which he commanded our forefathers to teach their children, so that the next generation would know them, even the children yet to be born, and they in turn would tell their children. Then they would put their trust in God and would not forget his deeds but would keep his commands (verses 1—7).

Now this was all well and good as long as those who were supposed to be passing on this vital information about God not only *did* pass it on but also believed in what they were passing on. But sadly as time went on, and even though more and more nations had been taught about Christianity, it seemed that less good biblical teaching was reaching the ears of the children.

In 1736 a children's worker was not born, but a prison reformer was. His name was Robert Raikes and he was a newspaper publisher by trade. He noticed that many young children who spent their lives working in factories were getting involved with crime, and he had a feeling that a lot of this was due to the fact that they were uneducated.

Realising that six days did they labour, the only day left to give them any sort of instruction was of course on Sunday.

It was in 1780 that his highly controversial Sunday school began, thanks to the support of an Anglican vicar and the dedication of many ordinary folk who opened up their homes to get the idea off the ground.

So this was how the house church movement began!

Their teaching was not all about Christianity, however. They covered a variety of basic subjects that they believed would be helpful to the children, hopefully keeping them out of trouble and ultimately out of prison.

Many church leaders, however, could not cope with this revolutionary idea. One of their main arguments was that the teaching was interfering with the proper Sunday observance. Even in this day and age Pharisees continued to make their presence felt by promoting the letter of the law and not understanding the spirit behind it.

Their other argument, which incenses me, was that they did not believe the poor children should be educated as they may become too intelligent, disagree with the way the country was being run and cause a revolution. The good old church leaders of the day, as insecure as ever, were retaining the motto of 'Keep the folk simple and nobody will be in a position to argue with our theological interpretations.' That's right: 'The less people know, the better off we will all be!'

Could there be a parallel today as to why we leave certain scriptures out, like Acts 2 and 1 Corinthians 12 to name but two, when we are teaching the children? Could this be because we are not only frightened that we will not be able to answer all their questions, but also that they may cause a minor revolution if they discover that some of what we teach as essential we do not carry out? To do so would cause a major rethinking and even a restructuring of our meetings...more than a leader's job is worth.

As you may have observed, though, Sunday schools did catch on, and they spread very quickly around the world. Before Raikes died it must have been a great encouragement to him that by 1803 a national Sunday School Union was founded. What he courageously pioneered had now become accepted as an institution.

Here we are some 200 years later. Children are not slumming it any more in factories; many are lazing around the home enjoying the luxury of the television and video age. Very few are uneducated. In fact, many have started on the long educational road by the age of three, and because all subjects are taught in our state schools, the church now confines itself to teaching just Religious Education, with varying amounts of sincerity and commitment depending on which church you attend.

So I am not being at all controversial when I make the statement: Sunday schools, rest in peace. You have had your day and done a grand job, but nowadays you are not relevant to the age we are living in. God has used you greatly in the past, but what does he want to use to affect our Christless generation today?

I am a firm believer that although the fundamentals of what we believe and who we believe in never change—Jesus Christ is the same, yesterday, today and for ever—the way in which we do things must be open to constant change and revision. The church should never be accused of being archaic, old-fashioned and outdated. We should not just wait for the unchurched to act and then re-act; we should be leading the way.

If we believe that Jesus provides life to the full—not the easiest life around, but certainly the most exciting and fulfilling—why aren't there more people who want to become Christians? One of the reasons is that we are caricatured as wimpy, weak-willed people; we are yesterday's people who, unlike the Lord Jesus, have little relevance to today and no relevance to for ever.

For them, to visit a church is like visiting a museum, where they would find an interesting variety of old relics whose greatest assets are that they keep themselves to themselves and portray how miserable life can be if you are not a non-Christian.

Sunday school is yet another page out of the history books.

Let us consider some major changes that may hopefully bring us more into the present.

Firstly, the name Sunday school for unbelieving children is meaningless and a joke. To our Christian children it is at best a total embarrassment. Can you put yourself in their position and at the age of fourteen expect them to witness to their friends and invite them to hear more about Jesus at Sunday school? They get enough persecution and intimidation without us adding to it by making them use a silly name.

Another reason for change is that a lot of children do not enjoy weekday school, especially as they grow older, and to have to tell their friends that they are going to school on Sundays as well is a big turn-off, both for Christian and also for the friend whom they are hoping to encourage along.

I can see some of you nodding your heads and agreeing with me, and you have changed the name to junior church.

I'm sorry, but in my opinion this is even worse than Sunday school. I believe that it is putting a confusing and unbiblical concept into children's minds. There is no such thing as a junior church in the Bible, or a senior one for that matter. The Bible talks about one true church, that is the body of believers. It is so easy for a child to imagine that if he is just part of junior church, he is not part of the real church, and it is only as he grows older and joins the main congregation that he becomes a significant and important member.

It is also very easy for adults to treat a junior church as inferior and to start believing that children are of less importance to Christ than they are.

No one would dare tell you, but just a small indication can be found of how leaders view the junior church if you compare how much of the church's finances go towards adults, compared with that which is set aside for the children's work. Or answer me this one; if the junior church and the senior church both had overhead projectors and the senior church's failed to work, would they have a right to take and use the junior church's projector? Most would say yes, because they see the senior church as more important than the junior church.

Now I know that I am only talking about names, but in this day and age names are important. They do need to be thought out and prayed about. Each church may have a different name for its children's work which is suitable to its locality. When you have thought up a name, however, do remember to get it endorsed by the children as they are going to be the ones who need to feel happy about using it as they make that personal invitation for their friends to join them.

What is the aim of our children's meetings? We need to have clear goals, otherwise if we try to do a bit of everything at every meeting, usually the children end up with a lot of nothing.

Let us begin with bible teaching. We must remember that we are teaching what the Bible actually says, and not what we would like it to say. There are a number of teaching aids produced by various organisations, which range from being very old-fashioned to very helpful. Before you decide to use one of these, do look around at all that is on offer, their emphasis can be quite different.

Now I have called these teaching 'aids', and that is all they are. They were never meant simply to be read out to the children, or to take the place of further research and preparation. Alongside these helps must come prayer and personal inspiration, otherwise the child will notice no difference between you and the teacher at school who so often just regurgitates a textbook.

You are not only sharing divine truth, but truth that has affected your life; your teaching is not theoretical words alone but a living experience.

Most important of all, you must communicate with the children. Truth, however important, needs to be delivered in a way which the listener will not only understand and be challenged by, but will also enjoy and remember. To do this you either need to use visual aids, or if you are of quite extrovert personality you can be a visual aid yourself and hold children's attention that way.

Let me share with you one way that I often use. I believe that the day of the *Jungle Doctor* stories, or even the concrete *Jungle Doctor* stories, are numbered as our main teaching emphasis. These are great for a child to read and enjoy as bedtime stories maybe, but our responsibility is to teach them the Bible.

It may be of some help if I share with you how I could prepare my talk. I would start by using a story that was not so well known. Parts of the Old Testament are great action-packed stories that although at first may seem to have little relevance to the New Testament, the more we study them the more we realise how much God has to teach us through them.

I would read this story at least six to a dozen times from different translations until it was firmly set in my memory. I would then go to Bible dictionaries and commentaries and follow any cross references to find out even more about the passage. By this time I have discovered the events before it, around it and after it, and have worked out its context.

Then, as I am not going to just read this story but live it out in front of the children and portray it in my own words in a way they will understand, I write down on a piece of card about fifteen headings so that if I do seize up with stage fright I can still glance down and hopefully continue.

There may also be a Scripture verse in the middle of the story that I would like them to learn. I would write this down again to make sure I get it right.

After all this I would have some idea as to how the Lord wanted to apply certain things to the children's lives. I would headline these at the bottom of my card.

While doing all this I would spend a lot of time praying about it. Even though it may end up being the best and most polished talk I have ever given, without the anointing of the Holy Spirit on myself and the talk will do little to change lives.

If you are not a very visual person, you will need to help the children's memories with visual aids. Personally, I feel that the good old flannelgraph should be returned to the soap bag because so many of the pictures are dated.

I praise the Lord that he is raising up some very gifted artists who are using their talents with great inspiration, and are not only equal to their modern-day non-Christian counterparts, but are even surpassing them.

I would sum up visual aids by saying that our children deserve the best, and the best is not always the most expensive, but usually it is. I find it exciting that new resources are regularly becoming available, but you will need to be a bit of a Sherlock Holmes to track them down.

As well as teaching the children Bible stories, we need to teach them how to talk to and listen to God. In another part of this book I have mentioned how to pray for others for healing, but the child needs to know first how God speaks and how he can speak to God.

A child needs to learn that it is not common for God to speak to him from heaven in a loud voice which his ears can hear, just as it is not the norm that God will appear before his very eyes in person. Yes, these may have happened to some, but we don't want our children thinking that unless this happens to them they have no chance of communication with God.

God's voice is a gentle voice that can reach our hearts via our eyes and minds as we read the Bible. It can be a louder voice as it passes through our hearts via the mouth of the preacher, or it can be a flash that hits our conscience then reaches our hearts. We can never tie God down to how he speaks—he even spoke through a donkey in the Bible. But we can be sure of a couple of things. The first is that what he says will never contradict the Bible, and the other is that when we are walking close to God his voice is unmistakable. Jesus said, 'My sheep hear my voice.'

When it comes to speaking to God, a child must always remember that it is Almighty God to whom he is speaking. Through teaching that Jesus is our best friend, our prayers sometimes become so over familiar that they are on the point of blasphemy; we must learn that real friendship demands real respect.

I do not teach name it and claim it, cash on demand, or trying to hold the Lord at ransom by saying, 'Do it now, or else.' I have no right to demand from God, but he is always available and has allowed me the privilege to talk to him and also to share with him my doubts, fears and questions. We must learn to come before God with a humble heart.

With both how to listen and how to speak to God, I've found that sharing some personal experience of doing things the right way and wrong way has been a great help to the children.

I have not covered songs and worship in this chapter because again they are covered elsewhere.

As I close, let me emphasise that it is important for children to spend time with their own age groups, just as in the previous chapter I emphasised how important it is that all ages of the family also meet regularly together.

We have a mid-week house group system for the adults of our fellowship, where they meet, learn, pray and share together, and we found that it was a natural progression to let our children also have mid-week house groups. They meet for an hour—usually six till seven—twice a month, in homes where they are taught about worship, the Bible, fruit and gifts of the Spirit, and so on, all in a very informal atmosphere. Then, on the two remaining weeks, we hire a large hall, and on one night have a games evening which is purely recreational, but hopefully teaching important lessons like how to be a good loser and not just a good winner.

It's best to forget about tagging on an epilogue. This is unnecessary as all the children present will also be attending the other three 'more spiritual' weeks throughout the month anyway.

On the other night we have a children's celebration, where we bring in a full music band, pull out all the stops and have a great evening of praising God together.

The children are encouraged to bring along their friends who are not Christians, but if these children come from non-Christian backgrounds, we not only keep a close link with the parents, informing them of what we are teaching their child, but also invite them around to special parents' evenings, not only get to know them better, but also because we want to see the whole family saved and not just the child.

In the previous chapter I explained that each week at my local fellowship the children and adults worship together on Sunday morning. We have found that by doing this we lose a lot less children than those who choose to separate the lambs from the sheep.

The largest proportion seem to drop away because they have learned how to become secure and 'top of the class' in their children's group, but when told that they must now progress up to 'the church meeting' they suddenly discover that they have forgotten what it was like and how to cope with being bottom of the pile. Many have never sat through or enjoyed an adult service and never really learned how to relate to adults, so being in this vulnerable position they feel

161

they cannot cope, and if they can't come to the children's meetings they won't come to anything.

Have you noticed that some children's groups still have eighteen-year-old men as their pupils? It's because they are too insecure to move on, and the leaders don't want to force them because they don't want to lose them. Yet another good reason for that regular Sunday morning all-age family service.

Finally, the house groups start for the six-year-olds and every few years they move with their friends to another home, where of course the teaching depth increases as their age and ability increase.

At the age of approximately fourteen or fifteen they spend a few weeks with one of the leaders on what we affectionately call 'The Foundation Course'. Here they are taught in detail the basics of what the fellowship believes and what we stand for (or maybe what we don't and won't stand for).

This completed, they are ready and equipped again to move on with their friends and to be welcomed into one of the adult house groups.

Although nothing is without its problems, this does work. We have tried to remove all major changes and upsets, and even joining the adults is not so difficult as not only are the house groups relaxed and fun, but they have already had a chance to get to know some of the oldies at the Sunday morning family service. Although it would be dishonest to say that no one ever leaves our fellowship, it is honest to say that we lose very few.

This may not be the answer to all your prayers, but I hope that it will be an answer to some.

11

Clipping Angels' Wings

When a child becomes a Christian, it is so often a case of, 'What do you want first, the good news or the bad news?' The good news is that the Bible teaches in 2 Corinthians 5:17: 'Therefore, if anyone is in Christ, he is a new creation; the old has gone, the new has come!'

The bad news is that the first time they join up with other Christians for a meeting they will discover that although they are new creations, the old is still here and the new has not only yet to come, but seems light years away. They will be taught that 'brand new people' must not only learn about 'old time religion' but must also learn how to live in it.

Please hear me out; I am not for one minute saying that all trappings and traditions are wrong and we should ban the lot of them. On the contrary, not only do many older folk enjoy them because of their upbringing, but they also find that they enhance their spiritual lives. The point I am making is, do we really need to inflict them on our up-and-coming generation of the twenty-first century?

Let me put in another way: history is important to where we are now, and it is valuable to look back and see how the Lord has moved us on with the times, but do we really want to be seen to the average non-believer to be living in the past and doing some very strange things which are not going to bring them any closer to the kingdom and are not the essentials that are taught in the Bible? Are we not wasting our children's time by teaching them things that bear no relevance to the Bible and their society, when we could be teaching them things that do? Are we going to lose many of these children in their teenage years, because they don't want to be associated with the Lord and Scripture, but more because they don't want to be aligned to religious traditions which they really have no desire to introduce to their unsaved friends.

For the rest of this chapter I want to look at a few of our traditions. Some are biblical but sadly have become ceremonious and very difficult for a child to understand, and others are ceremonious which we have to make biblical but don't particularly want our child to understand.

My observations are that all of the following have produced questions by children, and all need to be talked through and clarified in a very simple way to save them a lot of confusion later on in life. It is

important, however, that we as adults also seriously
think through the questions so that hopefully we will
have some answers and definitions for them that not
only make sense but are also biblical.

1 Clerical wear

I always looked forward to being ordained because I
knew that I was then entitled to wear a clerical collar.
This is better known as a dog collar or a ring of confidence. Apart from always enjoying dressing up, it also
got me noticed and everyone recognised that I was a
man of the cloth, even though wearing this did not
necessarily make me a man of God.

In every religion throughout the ages the 'spritual
leaders' have always chosen to dress differently from
Mr Average. There are two obvious reaons for this, the
first being, as I've just said, so that they can be recognised as a spiritual leader, and the other is the same
reason that policemen wear varying numbers of stripes
and different shaped hats, to show their ranking and
position.

To many children the church has become a joke, not
because of who we believe in but because of how our
leaders look. We know how the unsaved see the
church by their caricatures and cartoons of a short
balding man with strange spectacles and long robes
covering a large stomach. We have become the impres-
sionists' and comedians' dream, but personally I do
not find it very funny because at the end of the day
they are not only mocking the odd vicar, they are
subtly undermining our children's respect for the
church and its leaders.

It is worth noting, as we try and explain the place of
liturgical garb to our young people, that although the

priests in the Old Testament may have worn it, the Son of God did not. He chose to look like a normal person and that is why he so easily mixed with and related to ordinary people. The divine example showed both his leadership position and spirituality, not by the clothes he wore, but by who he was.

Also, it is a fact that the very early church leaders never bothered about dressing up and looking different, but with all the miraculous signs and wonders going on you couldn't really miss them, could you? They also were easily recognised as men of God.

It was when Emperor Constantine made Christianity a state religion in the fourth century, that the religious wardrobe became available. I am sure that it was more than just coincidence that at the time the church had become law and the initial fire was starting to be well controlled, the leaders started to look to clothing, not anointing, to portray their positions.

I have always tried to teach children the truth of 1 Samuel 16:7 which was referring to a young boy called David: 'The Lord does not look at the things man looks at. Man looks at the outward appearance, but the Lord looks at the heart.' Clothes and position are not things of great concern to God; what is important is how much you love him which is shown in how much you are obedient to him. Although I have met a lot of children who feel that in time God wants them to become leaders; and who may well benefit from theological training, unless they change their minds with age, very few would want to enter a denomination where dressing up is obligatory. They too see it as unnecessary.

2 Bible translations and paraphrases

I was looking through some new children's books a short while ago and was amazed to see that in a brand new edition, the scriptures quoted were in an 'olde worlde language' that had its heyday way back in the seventeenth century. When I asked the sales lady why that was, she told me she felt that it was vital to use this original archaic language, so that children could see that the Bible was different from any other book (which I'm sure would have blessed William Shakespeare who seemed to use a similar sort of verbiage).

What a strange argument. Here we are talking about God-breathed, inspired truth that has lasted near enough since the beginning of time, but to make it stand out from other books it needs to be written in old-fashioned English.

All I want is to see children reading and learning from the Bible. I am not too bothered which translation or paraphrase they use in their early years.

I was privileged to hear Dr Kenneth Taylor a short while ago and was knocked out by seeing what a wonderful and humble man of God he is. I've read some reviews of the Living Bible which hammered him and went as far as to say that a paraphrase like his could never be used by God. It was interesting to hear that the main reason it came into being was because as he spent time teaching his children they found the Authorised Version and the Revised Standard Version hard to read, so he put the Scripture into his own words in a way they could understand and appreciate. Now millions all over the world have benefited from its easy readable style.

Don't misunderstand me, I am not recommending that every parent now tries to be a Bible translator, but reading Scripture to a child from any translation does not necessarily mean that it is doing the child good. The child, like Philip's Ethiopian eunuch friend in the desert, needs someone to explain what the words actually mean.

At our wedding, when I knew that unsaved people were going to be present, I had to fight tooth and nail to get the minister to speak from the Living Bible and not the Authorised Version. That, I may hasten to add, was nothing to do with choosing a more accurate translation. It was just because it was his personal favourite version, which probably happened to be loose leaf and had his sermon notes in.

As I've grown older I've found that I prefer the New International Version. Likewise, with children, once they have an overall outline of Scripture from a paraphrase, they can then move on to a translation for greater accuracy; less browsing and more study. But again, don't expect them to go back to the 'thees and thous' translations for two reasons. The first is that when they quote Scripture to their schoolfriends they need to use today's language to be understood, and secondly, some of the modern translations are a lot more accurate than the 1611 favourite.

3 The church and the house of God

Children are very confused by both of these expressions, and we again need to teach them biblically what they mean and not what they have grown to mean throughout the generations.

The church of God consists of people, and never has been and never will be a building. The church is made up of all persons who have by the Holy Spirit been reborn into God's family and have been made new creatures in the Lord Jesus. The house of God is that same people; it is not a building. The Bible clearly tells us where God dwells: in his people.

In Acts 17:24 Paul says, 'The God who made the world and everything in it is the Lord of heaven and earth and does not live in temples built by hands.' He then says in 1 Corinthians 3:16–17: 'Don't you know that you yourselves are God's temple, and that God's Spirit lives in you? If anyone destroys God's temple, God will destroy him; for God's temple is sacred, and you are that temple.'

Yes, children need to be taught to respect buildings and property, and some of our older buildings are very beautiful and of great historic value. But they are not the church, and they are not the house of God. Children need to learn that to respect, love and care for each other is of far greater importance. There are adults who would love and care more for a building than they would their fellow man. We must set the example.

Biblically, the stone walls and hard wooden seats deserve no more 'reverential' treatment than a school hall or someone's living room, and it is bordering on idolatry to say that they do.

Teach children that they are a part of the church. Teach them that they are 'a house' of God because God lives in them. True, they are not *the* church or *the* house of God—they need to be with other believers to become that—but a church meeting can be held in a field, on the seashore or in a back garden. The building is of no relevance, unless of course it is raining.

4 Denominations

God has made us all very different, both adults and children. We enjoy different ways of expressing our praise and worship, we hold different emphases on different scriptures, and we have different forms of church government.

Children need to be taught that the church is the believers and not a denomination. I don't believe the Lord is too interested in whether we are Baptist, house church, Church of England or Brethren, but I know that he is interested in how much we love and honour each other.

Please do not encourage children to think that your denomination is the best and has all the answers. Teach them that although there are differences, all denominations have strengths and weaknesses and need to learn from each other.

There are two very different fellowships near us and it is very interesting to note that some of the leaders' teenagers have chosen to go to the other fellowship, not because they didn't like their dad leading, I would hasten to add, but because they felt more at home with the type of worship and structure of the other group. Their dads, being good leaders, didn't mind. They were just excited at the fact that their children were going on with the Lord.

As your children get older don't tie them down to denominational loyalty as this could be yet another way of losing them. Respect their differing views and opinions, even if their only motivation for change is that there are more people their age at the other place. Just be thrilled that they are going on with the Lord and meeting regularly with other Christians.

5 Tithes and offerings

A child sits and waits as a large plate or a nice little embroidered bag is passed along each row, with two men who could easily be employed by Securicor standing at each end of the row to keep the bag moving. Once the child has dropped the ten pence or two pence piece in, depending on how generous he feels, the two men walk to the back of the church until they get a nod from the leader at the front. Then, with a perfect sense of timing, they slowly and silently walk towards the front with all the precision of the Grenadier guards on a good day. This twice weekly ceremony is affectionately known as the 'march of the money-bags'. Here the money is prayed for, and that is the last time the child will see his ten pence or two pence piece. Where do they think it goes? Some believe that as it has been offered to God, he literally comes down from heaven and takes it back with him.

Children need to learn about giving, but so often they only get the two extremes. One extreme is where people take no thought about money, because everyone seems to have plenty, so they give the smallest amount of change they have in their pockets. The other is where the leader is practically in tears out at the front begging the people to give so that he can provide his family with a Sunday lunch.

Biblically the idea of giving a tenth is still very valid today, as this was first mentioned under Abraham to all people and was not just an instruction given to the Children of Israel by Moses. The only way that Jesus superseded it was by saying in Luke 14:33: 'Any of you who does not give up everything he has cannot be my disciple.'

I teach children that we in fact own nothing, because when we gave our lives to God, we also gave him everything we own. God, though, has allowed us to have possessions and money on loan, which we are to oversee and be good stewards of. Therefore, it is good training to give a tenth of our income or pocket money, but there will be times when God wants us to give more than this and even to share around some of our most treasured possessions. I then go on to explain that this should be no big deal as I have already taught them that all we have is God's, so it is just giving back to him what he already owns. The Bible instructs us that it is also important to give cheerfully. So many times I have told those collecting the money to accept nothing from anyone unless they are smiling. This of course is a heartbreaking exercise to the church treasurer. Generally he is more concerned about receiving big cheques than seeing big grins.

I also teach that our local fellowship and leaders do not live on thin air, and as they are not only caring for us but spending many hours with the local community, we have a responsibility to help support them and their families. I would say a tenth of their pocket money is not a lot to give, especially when they see what they get in return.

I remember a young teenager arguing with her friend over tithing. Her friend insisted that she could not afford to give that amount of money, and the young teen replied that she could not afford not to give. She had learned that as she gave, she actually received. Children need to be taught that giving must come from the heart, and incidentally the way to a man's heart is not through his stomach, it's through his wallet.

6 Baptism

I have always considered that the many hours of debate people have over the amount of water one should be baptised in is missing the whole point of baptism.

The whole of the New Testament points to the fact that we should believe and then be baptised. We are making a statement before God and before everyone listening that we have finished with the old sinful life, thus burying it, and have now risen again with our Lord Jesus to live out a brand new clean life as a brand new cleaned-out person.

At what age then should children be baptised? This is a very hard question and I am not sure if I know the answer to it. My personal feelings are that both salvation and being filled with Holy Spirit do require a response from the child, but they are both gifts from God. They don't need to understand everything that is taking place; a lot of what is happening will be revealed to them as they grow older and get to know God and Scripture better.

With believer's baptism there is a difference. The person being baptised is not stating his death and resurrection through the eyes of faith, it is a thought out, understood commitment that he is making. So although I would not dare to put an age limit on it, I do believe that it has to be a response from the child, not the parent or children's worker, and that child needs to understand the words he is saying and the commitment he is making.

By the way, there is nothing in the Bible that says it has to be a leader or ordained man doing the baptising. I am looking forward to the day when Christian parents baptise their own children; this would solve a lot of problems because, with their leaders' approval and before all the congregation, they are taking the responsibility for their own children which is the way it should be.

7 Communion or breaking of bread

Again this wonderful feast of remembrance and thanksgiving should never exclude believing children, but it does need explaining to them in a very simple way.

Teach them that it is not the bread and the wine that is holy or anything special; it is that you are remembering the pain and the agony that the Lord Jesus went through so that we could be made right with him. Explain that we have an illustration in front of us: the bread being the body of Christ that was beaten, and the wine being his blood that was shed to make us clean. Explain that this is no morbid feast and that we are not cannibals or vampires. To some children who have been allowed to watch horror films these thoughts seriously come into their minds when eating the body or drinking the blood are mentioned. Tell them it's a time to remember what Jesus went through and to be thankful that he not only died, but he rose again from the dead and is one day returning to earth so that we can be with him for ever.

If at all possible it's best that parents sit with their children, or take responsibility for any young friends they have brought along, while this is done in a meeting. This way they can explain what is happening. It needs to be made very clear, though, that this is a special feast for believers. This should not be taken lightly and just given to every child.

The breaking of bread should not only take place within the confines of a meeting; we as a family have enjoyed just sitting in the countryside with some bread and drink and giving thanks to Jesus for all he has done for us.

Let me finish by saying again that this need not be a solemn time, but it certainly is a sacred one and must be taken with true respect and reverence. We must impress on our children that this, above most things, is no joke—they must not take it lightly—but as the invitation to come and join in this remembrance feast has been given by the Lord Jesus himself, they must not be frightened to accept the invitation and to come, eat, drink and be thankful.

As I mentioned earlier, let's stick to teaching the children what the Bible teaches. It will take them all of their lives on earth to learn just some of that. Any unnecessary stuff we try to include, although it may not be outwardly harmful, will prove distracting and a waste of time in an age where the Spirit of God has so many vital things to teach these young ones. Please, hold on to the old if you want to, but don't try to pass it on to the new generation.

12

Angels' Ancestors

It was he [Jesus] who gave some to be apostles, some
to be prophets, some to be evangelists, and some to
be pastors and teachers, to prepare God's people for
works of service, so that the body of Christ may be
built up until we all reach unity in the faith and in the
knowledge of the Son of God and become mature,
attaining to the whole measure of the fulness of Christ
(Eph 4:11–13).

I wonder why we wait until a child is an adult before
we start encouraging him and helping him to develop
his ministry? So often we do not recognise children's

God-given talents until they are older, and by then we may well have missed out because they have left the church anyway.

One of the functions of any leader is to see what qualities his people have, and this needs to include the qualities that children possess. Many feel that future leaders for their local fellowships will be imported when needed, but I'm a keen believer that the vast majority of our future local ministries are sitting in our children's meeting waiting to be trained and discipled.

Generally, people are not allowed to develop nowadays. Unless they have an incredible natural inbuilt talent and can preach immediately, they are rarely given the chance to develop. We leaders forget all too quickly how green and inexperienced we were when we first started, and often wait for up and coming leaders to be as we are now, not as we were then, before we can accept them.

I remember when I gave my very first talk. I was given that bit of freedom to do something, and it was awful, but people didn't give up on me, they trained me. Everyone in a fellowship must have a God-given talent somewhere to bless the body of Christ with, and all leaders have to do is find it. The problem is, if it is that hard for an adult to find and be allowed to develop his ministry, what hope do our children have?

There is no age limit for any ministry at either end of the scale, but the sooner one is encouraged to start, the more chance one has of being proficient when one is older.

One of the great unwritten laws of the church seems to be, 'You've got to prove yourself,' but no one is really sure what that means. I think this statement means that you have not proved yourself until you have done something absolutely fantastic and everyone is 100 per cent behind you and thinks you are great. But how often does that happen in those early days?

Even in your local church situation you are always going to find people who do not like you very much. Oh, they love you because the Bible says they must, but they don't particularly like you. And also, due to the fact that you have grown up in the church, they still see you as a young boy or girl, even when you are middle-aged. Some folk will never see you as anything, and it is so easy after a bit of criticism to become discouraged.

Church leaders need to release people into their ministries and even allow them to make mistakes. They can cover all this as long as the pupil is humble, submissive and willing to learn.

Don't you find that there is always someone better at what you are doing in the church? Is there someone better at children's work than you? If there is, that person only arrived at that point through learning and doing it. Why wait until a child becomes an adult before we give him that opportunity? If you work with children you need to start promoting their talents. Keep your eyes open and begin looking for certain things the children are good at.

You need to watch for tell-tale signs, indicating what kind of gift or talent there is. Little Johnny might pick up a guitar and only play one chord, but that's a beginning. Don't spread it around, but a lot of my own songs only use another two, and he should certainly be up to my standard in no time.

Others might be more percussive, so you will need to encourage them in that and let them have a tam-

179

bourine at some stage. It's better to hand one tambourine out to a child with a sense of rhythm, than twenty out to children with no sense of timing.

Someone may be good at art. Perhaps you were disgusted that he was doodling during your talk, but then to your amazement, before you screw up his masterpiece and throw it in the bin, you notice that it has shades of a budding Van Gogh. Use him! Just think, it will save you having to do the artwork and posters that you so hate doing. Promote his qualities.

It maybe necessary to visit the children's homes to find out what they are capable of doing. It's a great opportunity, especially to get to know unsaved parents. On a different level, as 1 Corinthians 12 reminds us, although we may all be able to speak in tongues, prophesy, pray for healing, do a bit of admin, and so on, there are those who have a specific ministry to the church and will major in one particular area, but they will still need help and encouragement.

You need to praise their qualities. We spend too much time talking about the bad things children do: 'They're scruffy and they sneeze all the time. They never clap, never sing—and they always have their hands in their pockets.' Too much negative, and so little positive.

If you examine their characters, you will see some good qualities and some fantastic fruit. There will be gentleness in some, indicating a pastoral future; a real kindness in others which will be shown in later years as a ministry of hospitality.

We must help the children discern what their ministries are. We don't know how long they have on this earth, so let's start to encourage them while they are here.

We can learn much from some of the famous 'children' of the Bible. Unfortunately, you never know how old the child was because the word 'children' sometimes related to thirty-four-year-olds. But here are a few heroes who we know were learning and being prepared for their future while they were very young.

An obedient son

> Isaac spoke up and said to his father Abraham, "Father"?
>
> "Yes, my son?" Abraham replied.
>
> "The fire and wood are here," Isaac said, "but where is the lamb for the burnt offering?"
>
> Abraham answered, "God himself will provide the lamb for the burnt offering, my son." And the two of them went on together.
>
> When they reached the place God had told them about, Abraham built an altar there and arranged the wood on it. He bound his son Isaac and laid him on the altar, on top of the wood. Then he reached out his hand and took the knife to slay his son (Genesis 22:7–10).

We don't know how old Isaac was, but he was reasonably young. The story obviously gives credit to Abraham, but I want to give credit to Isaac. I think it's amazing.

Let's try to picture what was actually happening. Isaac knew his father loved him and is invited to go with his dad to perform a sacrifice. They go away from home to do it, and after quite a while they get to the top of a mountain where they are to give their offering up to God. I can imagine young Issac's excitement.

But as Isaac stands there, he finds himself getting tied up, still not having been told what or where the animal was that they were going to sacrifice. It suddenly must have hit him, 'I am the sacrifice. Dad is going to kill me.'

If it had not been of God, that boy would have been filled with every fear imaginable! He did not fight and kick, but I also guarantee that he did not particularly want to die. Isaac was a special young man, already showing the unique, inbuilt quality of a man of God, even in his early years. Isaac was obedient to God, but it didn't all just happen there and then on that mountain top; I believe he had been well trained and was well taught as to who Father God was. If God said it, it had to be right., even though he may not have understood why. At the same time I am sure that all sorts of questions would have gone through his mind as his dad prepared him for sacrifice.

Isaac was also an obedient servant to his father. He had a fantastic servant heart and trusted his father's guidance implicitly. He believed in his father. How many children today believe or trust in their parents—even in simple things? It's little wonder that some find it hard to trust Father God as they get older.

The boy prophet

Samuel lay down until morning and then opened the doors of the house of the Lord. He was afraid to tell Eli the vision, but Eli called him and said, "Samuel, my son."

Samuel answered, "Here I am."

"What was it he said to you?" Eli asked. "Do not hide it from me. May God deal with you, be it ever so severely, if you hide from me anything he told you."

So Samuel told him everything, hiding nothing from him. Then Eli said, "He is the Lord; let him do what is good in his eyes" (1 Samuel 3:15–18).

I find the story of Samuel very exciting. We know Samuel was a young boy. You may remember how Hannah actually brought him to the temple and gave him over to God when he was tiny. For a young lad that must have been quite something to be handed over like that. He had no choice in the matter, but God's hand was upon it, and his mum, with the confirmation of the priest, knew that she was acting in obedience to Father God.

God's hand is on our children as well. It's no use saying, 'Ah well, God's hand was more on those children in those days,' because that is just not true.

Samuel had learned to live without parents. In your work with children, you will have plenty of people excusing a youngster's behaviour because he or she came from a bad background or a broken home. They conclude that because of such a background, the child is going to be disadvantaged and will therefore find spiritual things more difficult to grasp. But that needn't be true. My wife, Irene, came from an extremely rough and tragic background, from a child right into her late teens, and God totally transformed her and healed her of all that. Her life is a tremendous testimony of God's power and grace.

As mentioned in previous chapters, there may well be some things that you will need to pray through with a child who comes from a tragic home situation, but ultimately he or she has as much chance as any other. Samuel would have known nothing about home life and yet the temple was where God wanted him to be.

If people come to you and say that there is a reason for a certain child's behaviour, again that child might need to be shown more love, but he has as much chance and potential to be used by God as any other child. The minute he feels he is different, he will start to act differently, and more often than not in a negative way.

Samuel heard the voice of God but didn't understand whose voice it was. Poor old Samuel had a rough night and little sleep; God was not going to leave him alone until he recognised his voice, which was going to be the most important thing in his life as he grew up to be a prophet.

Eli, though, actually taught him how to respond to God's voice, and showed him what to say. Likewise we need to teach our children what the voice of God sounds like and how to respond to it. Without instruction and guidance they can easily become confused and mistake God's voice for either their own ideas or worse still that of the deceiver, Satan himself.

I love the way Samuel prophesied. You can imagine this little lad sharing God's word. The boy spoke out what God was saying, even though it was bad news. He wasn't exactly sharing, 'God is with you; God is happy.' He had a message that was going to be a severe rebuke to Eli. Mind-blowing, isn't it, that God chose a young inexperienced little boy to tell one of the nation's spiritual leaders that he hadn't been obedient to God and would be punished. We need to be aware that God can still move a child to deliver such a message.

As we read through the biblical account, we can see that from that point on, Samuel was respected. From early days you can see the prophetic ministry developing in this young lad. And again, with some of our children today, we should be able to see a prophetic edge in their young lives.

My personal observation is that the prophectic ones sometimes tend to be a little rough, wild, and, dare I say it, outwardly rebellious, but somehow if you can see through that tough exterior you will find someone whose heart is really after God. We need to let the children speak God's word and share what is on his heart. Yes, us oldies will have to weigh it up, but they must have the opportunity to contribute.

Young heart after God

> So he asked Jesse, "Are these all the sons you have?"
> "There is still the youngest," Jesse answered, "but he is tending the sheep."
> Samuel said, "Send for him; we will not sit down until he arrives."
> So he sent and had him brought in. He was ruddy, with a fine appearance and handsome features.
> Then the Lord said, "Rise and anoint him; he is the one."
> So Samuel took the horn of oil and anointed him in the presence of his brothers, and from that day on the Spirit of the Lord came upon David in power (1 Samuel 16:11–13).

David had no fear. He was a boy who seemed to enjoy fighting with wild animals. The Bible actually says he went out of his way to fight bears! He was a warrior from the word go. That was in his heart. He was out there learning how to protect his dad's flock, and God knew that in a few years' time he would be the greatest protector of his flock the Children of Israel would ever know.

He also had persistence. Although still very young, he wasn't put off by his brothers, Goliath, or even King Saul. David knew God; he was and would remain God's friend. David's ambition was not to be the big hero. He just wanted to stand up for God. Where did he learn all about that? Obviously he learned from his dad and family; it would have been too late to learn about it on the battlefield while face to kneecap with a giant.

I believe he was a spiritual boy. This sort of God-filled courage did not come instantly; it came from a well-taught background. Goliath was just the chance he had been waiting for to put his teaching and faith into action.

Fear just wasn't present in David's heart. He had not considered losing because he knew that God was on his side. Some children think that every time they go to school and church, they cannot win. They lose their persistence and become frightened of all sorts of things, and end up living their lives as failures.

We are talking about more-than-conquerors, victorious-type Christianity, which the Lord Jesus has provided. They should not have their faces to the ground, but should be taught to hold their heads up high, confident and secure in the God they serve.

A little boy and a big giant; a little stone and a big victory; a little shepherd boy who grew into a great king.

The incredible dreamer

> Joseph, a young man of seventeen, was tending the flocks with his brothers, the sons of Bilhah and the sons of Zilpah, his father's wives, and he brought their father a bad report about them.

186

> Now Israel loved Joseph more than any of his
> other sons, because he had been born to him in his
> old age; and he made a richly ornamented robe for
> him. When his brothers saw that their father loved
> him more than any of them, they hated him and
> could not speak a kind word to him.
>
> Joseph had a dream, and when he told it to his
> brothers, they hated him all the more (Genesis 37:2–
> 5).

I think Joseph was incredible. I have such great respect for him. He knew what a dream from God was. While Samuel learned the audible sound of God's voice, Joseph knew God's voice in dreams. He not only knew when a dream was from God, but he also knew how to interpret it. He was far from perfect, however, and in those early years, he was also a little unwise.

One of the things you will notice when working with children, is they have not been gifted with great wisdom. Wisdom is something which comes from maturity. But just because they may sometimes go beyond their briefing from God, that is still no reason to stop or quench them.

We have to be patient with children because they will learn. I don't think Joseph was very wise. His dream wasn't a great blessing to his brothers, and there seemed very little need to tell them, even though what he was saying proved to be true.

Children need to be taught that when God speaks to them, on most occasions they will need to share what God has said, but there will be times when what God says is personal and, like Mary, Jesus' mother, they need to hold it in their hearts, keep it to themselves and not share it.

Joseph also coped with hatred and jealousy against him. It is very hard for a child to cope with these things, but he did. He was a very lonely child, which was not helped by having a father who spoiled him and treated him better than he did his other sons.

Whatever his brothers thought of him, however, Joseph was keen to see them, and was pleased when his dad told him to go and find them.

Imagine being grabbed, beaten up and thrown down a well. If the slightest thing happens to some people nowadays we not only sympathise with them, but we tend to believe they will be dogged by rejection for the rest of their lives. But here was a young lad suffering at the hands of murderous brothers. That was serious stuff for a little boy, but with all the horrendous fears that he must have felt as he was sold and dragged off to a foreign land, he refused to die of rejection. The voice of God had told him that he had a future, and whatever men might do to him, he was going to hang onto God's words, because he had been taught that they always come true.

Some so-called mature Christians today act like babies. You have only to shout 'Boo!' and make them jump and they claim to have a spirit of fear! They could learn so much from Joseph.

What a difference it makes if we teach our children that not only does God have a future for them, but the church has one too. If they have something to aim for, they can face all sorts of difficulties in life because they know that ultimately God has his hand on them, and they are given the boldness and power to fulfil that mission.

I remember taking a meeting where a little boy was crying his eyes out. Later he told me why. He said,

'God has just shown me he will use me in a ministry of music.' That young lad knew it was God speaking to him and that God has just given him a glimpse of his future, and not just how much fun it would be either.

On another occasion, an eleven-year-old boy said to me that God showed him he should be pursuing a preaching ministry. I heard later that the lad started preaching at his church's youth group and that he was brilliant.

At our fellowship we have yet to allow the young ones to lead the meetings, but we recognise they are showing promise. From a very young age they are encouraged to give children's talks in front of all ages.

We need to start looking for the little ministries springing up in children's lives, and then supply the right conditions for them to grow. Most of the Bible heroes were being trained in various avenues of ministry long before they became 'famous' for it. A ministry will take time to mature so the sooner you start training, the longer time the person will have on this earth to be used in it. Pride was once a problem with children. Now so many have so little self-worth that they are under the impression they can't do anything. With God's help we need to change that way of thinking.

Finally, if we do not allow children to develop their God-given talents for kingdom use, they will have to have an outlet and try to be successful in something. Sadly, they are likely to pursue personal ambition or making money, and surround their lives with priorities that will end up taking them away from God. Encourage their qualities, make and train up disciples, and let's enrich the church with their potential. Use them, or lose them.

13

Angels Unafraid

In the Bible there is the story of Elisha and his servant who discover that their house is surrounded by an Aramean army who have come to capture them. A very human petrified servant shouts in panic to his master, 'Oh my lord, what shall we do?' Elisha, being the mature prophet of God that he was, seemed amazingly cool, calm and collected about the whole situation. In fact the only answer he gave was, 'Don't be afraid...Those who are with us are more than those who are with them' (2 Kings 6:16).

I picture this poor young servant scratching his head, and although he may not have been the most

191

mathematically intelligent servant in the world, every time he counted himself and his master there was no way he could get beyond the number two. Yet there facing him, peering up at his window, was a large army.

Seeing his poor confused servant and wanting to put his mind at rest, Elisha then prayed to God and asked him to open his eyes so that he would be able to see. It was then that the servant's immense fear left him. He took his eyes off the human and physical dilemma and realised that he had nothing to be afraid of, because in the hills he saw God's army of horses and chariots of fire surrounding them, just in case protection was needed, which of course in this case it wasn't. God and Elisha had no trouble dealing with the situation.

Jesus reminds us in John 14:26–27:

> But the Counsellor, the Holy Spirit, whom the Father will send in my name, will teach you all things and will remind you of everything I have said to you. Peace I leave with you; my peace I give you. I do not give to you as the world gives. Do no let your hearts be troubled and do not be afraid.

Then Jesus talked about how the world would hate his disciples, but he also encouraged them by telling them about the work of the Holy Spirit and how the disciples' grief would turn to joy. He concluded chapter 16 by saying:

> I have told you these things so that in Me you may have perfect peace *and* confidence. In the world you have tribulation *and* trials *and* distress *and* frustration; but be of good cheer—take courage, be confident,

certain, undaunted—for I have overcome the world.
—I have deprived it of power to harm, have
conquered it [for you] (Jn 16:33, Amplified Bible).

If that does not encourage the most heavy hearted,
nothing will.

Fears are strange. Everyone has a fear of something,
and while some learn to live with these, others feel
they either need prayer for them or they need to con-
quer the fears themselves.

I believe that so often fear is the opposite to trust,
and the last thing that God wants is for his children to
live under its domination and for it to rule their lives. It
is one of the greatest means the evil one will use to
convince us that we are cowards and wimps and far
from being more than conquerors and the victorious
Christians that, thanks to the Lord Jesus, we should
be.

Maybe it would be good to have a look at a few
types of fears. The first fear is one that is definitely not
wrong and not sent to distract us, and that is 'holy
fear'. This fear comes from God and helps people to
not only hold in reverence his authority and to obey
his laws, but also encourages people to hate all forms
of evil. It is taught so often in the Old Testament, and
it never became outdated, because in the New Testament we find that the young Christians were taught to
'walk in the fear of the Lord'. To fear God did not
mean to live in terror of him; we know the Bible gives
great emphasis to God being loving and forgiving.

An approximate quotation from *Vines Expository Dictionary* tells us that the Greek word for fear of God
signifies firstly caution, then reverence (godly fear). It
continues by describing it as 'that mingled fear and

love which, combined, constitute the piety (devoutness) of man towards God; the Old Testament places its emphases on the "fear", the New Testament on the "love", though there was love in the fear of God's saints in Old Testament times, as there must be fear in their love today.'

Nice one, Mr V. I couldn't have put it better myself!

It is vitally important that children learn that Jesus is their best friend, but it is also important that they do not treat him in the casual way that they treat their best friend. The old saying of 'familiarity breeds contempt' is still a good one. We must teach our children that our best friend Jesus is Almighty God, and they do need to be careful about what they say to him and about him. Christians are sometimes rightly accused of being irreverent, whereas non-Christians are the ones who are blasphemous. Is there really any difference between these two words? A child wouldn't think so.

Children need to be taught that reverence is part of their true love for God, and far from inhibiting or restricting their frienship, it will enhance it and lead them deeper into a real and true relationship with the One they have chosen to serve and to follow.

The next fear is not a bad fear; it is one that I would call caution. When we instruct children that they must fear nothing, there are things that we want them to be sensible about.

When I was a teenager I did crazy things. I had no fear of getting hurt or dying; because I was young and reckless these things never crossed my mind. I was convinced that my innings down on this earth were at least three score years and ten, and, with a bit of good fortune, hopefully a bit longer. The rock band called 'The Who' wrote a cheerful little song called 'My Generation', and one of the lines went: 'I hope I die before I get old.' The drummer of the band, Keith Moon, was the only one who lived up to the lyrics and managed to die a relatively short while after the song became a smash hit. The songwriter and lead guitarist Pete Townshend, however, is still well and truly alive, and, dare I say it, getting rather old.

Pete Townshend wrote this song when he was young, wild and reckless to a generation that largely felt the same way, but Pete and his generation, as they creep into their forties and fifties, are not only a lot more cautious and careful nowadays, but would instruct the younger ones to be the same. Most have discovered that it wasn't quite so bad growing old, and are quite thankful that they are not dead.

We instil certain fears in our children because we want to protect them. We tell them that they must not talk to strange men and people they don't know, or get a lift in someone's car, however friendly they seem to be, because it is not safe.

We tell them not to touch plugs, cookers, certain dogs, fires, bleach, nettles, bees, wasps, slugs, paint, weedkiller, matches, fireworks, knives, razor blades, chisels, hammers, sewing machines, kettles, the hot tap, ink bottles, shoe polish, worms, toilets, glass, china, plus millions of other items.

We instruct them that they must not open the door to strangers for fear of thieves, answer the phone for fear of obscene phone calls, play with keys and locks in doors for fear of being locked in or out, open the upstair windows for fear of falling out, have the bath too full with water for fear of drowning, have the music too loud for fear of going deaf, play on the grass for fear of what they might tread in—again, just a tip of the iceberg of the actual fears that we have, and that we want our children to share with us.

It is a fact that we do pass on these fears. Let me explain. I remember seeing a little girl knocked down by the car in front of me. From that time on I had this mental picture of it being my child, and I was quite obsessive when teaching them road safety. Another time on a Christian holiday we were climbing up Snowdon in North Wales when one of the worst gales I had ever encountered hit us as we were halfway up the mountain. As ladies in the party were screaming and crying, I grabbed hold of my two boys, and although I tried to look brave, I don't mind admitting that I was scared stiff that they might come to harm. I tried to put them off climbing after that.

Through a bad experience, my wife Irene had a fear of large dogs, and quite naturally she always taught Suzy to be wary of them. Both of them wouldn't mind if they never saw a dog again and would think twice before accepting an invitation to go to tea with someone who had a lovely cuddly large Alsatian or Rottweiler waiting to welcome them.

Teaching children caution is vital in today's society, and passing on our fears to our children is inevitable.

Some minor fears will be grown out of, some will be humanly conquered, while others seem to make up our personality and make little or no difference to us. Small fears can be tolerated, but if the minor develops into the major, if what once sent a little shiver starts to get you shaking, if any fear starts to take a stronghold in a Christian's life, this is another story. Read on.

The third type of fear that I will mention is the evil fear; the one you are not in control of. It has gained control over you; it has made you its slave and is seriously in opposition with 'the great and mighty warrior' that God has called you to be. Christians should not, and do not have to, live with these, and either through their own prayers or somebody else praying for them, need to ask God to deliver them from these mantraps of the enemy.

These fears enter us through various ways and means, and sadly can have a devastating effect on children.

Children cannot always be blamed for their fears. Some of the saddest cases have been when they have in fact been the victims and understandably have allowed certain fears to be part of them. A child who has been molested will often have a fear of adults, and many feel unclean and do not want any physical contact. A child who has been excessively beaten will cower if you just raise your hand while near him. There are many such tragic and extreme cases, and they are growing in numbers, even in Christian homes. As depressing as this might seem, the good news is that Jesus can and will perfectly heal and restore these little ones if they will allow him to. It has been so exciting to see this happen so many times when this evil fear has been commanded to leave in the name of Jesus.

Most fears in children are self-inflicted. A lot of fears seem to enter through the window of the soul: the eye. Films and videos can be wonderful tools of the enemy. It's expected that the eighteen-certificate films when shown to young ones will have a detrimental effect, and, of course, they usually do. Whether it's the bloody horror of the reality of war, or the fictitious horror of a fantasy hero who has to kill everybody in a brutal fashion, especially communists, to save the world, it's not long before children can see these figures lurking in every woodland and behind every tree, and in comes their fear of going out, especially on their own.

The original 'screamy' horror movies have progressed into the supernatural, and now children not only have a fear of big houses, ghosts and the dark, but they are also given the Hollywood interpretation of the devil, occult, demon possession and the messy business of exorcism.

If adults want to fill their minds with this sort of rubbish and live with the consequences, I suppose that is up to them, but what really makes me mad is that some of these subjects have had a bit of humour added to them, given a good musical score, and are now being made specifically for our children who can watch them on television at peak family viewing time.

I have prayed for hundreds of children who have innocently watched these sorts of films and found they can't forget certain gruesome sequences, or have recurring nightmares.

So-called children's programmes can provide more fears in a child's life than many adult ones, so that is why the programmes our children watch need to be prayerfully and carefully selected.

We must remember that every child will be susceptible to different fears; they are not all scared by the same things. I remember we had to pray for one little girl who had a real fear of water after watching the film *Jaws*. Yet I know many children who have watched that same film and suffered no adverse effects. Someone else saw *Mary Poppins* and, after seeing all those chimney sweeps dancing on a roof and then coming down the chimney, had a real fear of people climbing down her chimney.

I do not mean to be a killjoy. I spend many happy hours watching television and videos, but it is a parent's responsibility to find out the vulnerable spots in their children, especially when they are very young, and do their best to keep them away from them.

I've mentioned television, but don't forget to keep your eyes on books, comics and magazines (especially computer magazines), computer games, and most definitely any role-playing games such as Dungeons and Dragons which encourage the mind to play on the more sinister and dark side of life and give room for fears to start to dominate.

I must make it clear that with major fears, time is not the healer, God is. If left and not dealt with they will remain with that person right the way through their lives, and no doctor's prescription or psychiatric help will be able to cure them, although temporary relief may be found through nicotine or alcohol, tranquillisers and sleeping tablets. However, no Christian in his right mind (excuse the pun) would ever see any of these as God's answer to fears.

To finish this chapter, let us have a look at how we can pray for these fears in our children and see them go once and for all.

As with healing, gentleness and simplicity in our ministering are the two important factors. It is unnecessary to lay big adult hands on small children's heads, and if you use a loud voice and shout as you pray, you are very likely to put more fear into that child than you are actually getting out.

For tinies, again as with physical healing, it is fine to pray over them while they are asleep. For older ones confession is often needed. When children talk to Father and say sorry that they watched this or read that, it helps them see that it was wrong, and also shows them from that moment onwards that they must try not to fall into the same trap again. Obviously where a child has been abused there may be nothing to confess, but if there is hatred towards a parent, this will need dealing with.

After confession, I break the hold of that fear in the child's life in the name of Jesus, and pray for the peace of God to fill the gap where the fear had been. Then I get the child to name that fear and tell it that because he belongs to the Lord Jesus it has no right to be part of him. Then I get the child in his own words to tell that fear to leave him. After this we praise God together, and what a wonderful experience to see one of these young ones, who seconds ago looked so heavy, now fully released and shining with the joy that only God can give.

This is not pie-in-the-sky stuff; this is reality. I have seen hundreds, if not thousands, prayed for in this way, and have seen God move in and perform a miracle that no amount of auto-suggestion or manipulation could achieve. And the proof that it was God was that it lasted and the children really did lose those fears.

Here are just a few of the prayers that the children wrote, some before their fears were dealt with, and some after. Remember as you read them that although some of these fears may seem trivial to you, they were far from that for the child who had them.

(1) Please, God, help me not to be frightened of AIDS. Now, God, take this fear out of me.

(2) I am no longer frightened of the hound of the Baskervilles.

(3) Dogs, and I'm afraid of nobody noticing me because of my eczema.

(4) [A *Jaws* watcher.] I was afraid of sharks. I kept thinking that they were in the swimming pool. Now I am not afraid.

(5) Lord, please help me not to be scared of being killed in the night.

(6) I'm not frightened, in the name of Jesus, of hearing footsteps in the bathroom and the water pipes clanking.

(7) I am not frightened of world wars, burglars and my teacher.

(8) I am no longer frightened of *Ghostbusters* and cracking my head open.

(9) I am not frightened of things on the floor and things that are on my dressing table. I am frightened of things in the air like clothes in my cupboard as they look as if they are moving.

(10) I will stop having nightmares, and I will stop watching late night movies.

(11) I was prayed for my fear of illness and now all the scabs on my fingers have all gone. Praise the Lord. [Yes I remember it well; it happened instantly.]

(12) Fear of dying of blindness.

(13) My brother has leukaemia and his is ill and I think you know what I am scared of and I do pray that the Lord Jesus will make him better.

(14) Lord, you know that I was scared of running fast because of my accident when I was young. Now it is no longer part of me.

(15) If someone is killed my age, I think that I'll die like that. When I was prayed for my fear seemed to come down my body and out of my toes.

(16) I am afraid that my mum will have a fit when I am on my own with her.

(17) Thank you for taking away my fear about being killed in a car, aeroplane or boat.

(18) Fear of getting water inside my head and dying.

(19) I was scared when people talked about witches and things like that.

(20) I am afraid of the dark, but Father God loves me and cares for me so I have nothing to fear.

(21) I am full of fear when I walk to school on my own, and kidnappers.

(22) I am afraid of people snatching me when I am in bed.

14

Angels' Guardians

So much that I have written in this book I have deliberately aimed at the parent/guardian and the children's worker, and although at times I may have given advice to the parent, this can often overlap to the children's worker, especially where the one-parent family needs some assistance, or the child is from a non-Christian home. I've tried to emphasise that the parent must have overall responsibility for that child, and the children's worker, however much love he or she may have for that child, has no right to feel that while the child is in their care they are adopting him.

I must repeat again that children's workers should be those who have been given a special talent from God which allows them to communicate, in a very clear yet profound way, biblical truths and their modern-day application to children.

They must encourage Christian parents to train the children in spiritual ways, and must not look down on them if the parents don't do their teaching according to the children's workers' manual, if there ever was such a thing. The parent and children's worker form a team, and there must be no competition between them as they they both want to see the child grow in the Christian faith. The parent is like the cake bearing both the spiritual and the day-to-day responsibilities, and the children's worker is like the icing on the cake, that something special, the treat, that will be of great benefit to the children and a great encouragement to the parents.

As well as overseeing the children's work in my local fellowship, I also run an international children's work called the Glorie Company. Glories are characterised as little smiling people who have springs instead of legs because they enjoy bouncing around a bit, large tambourines, and even larger smiles on their faces. Although they are fun characters, they love praising God, and their aim in life is to put him first, and not only be obedient to what he asks them to do, but also to do those things with a cheerful heart, not because they have to, no, it's because they want to, because they love him.

Although children can associate with these little characters, I have also found that teenagers and adults have adopted them too. This could be due to the many thousands of records and books that we have sold about them which I have tried to make appealing to all ages of the family.

For both local and national work I have had to be involved in selecting workers to join my team. Sometimes this has meant finding up to 100 for one event, but I have learned a lot in the process. I would like to share with you some of the qualities that I look for in a children's worker, and hopefully this will not only be a help to those who oversee the children's work, but also to those who are pondering whether this is what God is leading them into.

I must add that I don't expect all my workers to be brilliant in all the following, but I do expect them to be willing to learn and to be submissive to me as a team leader, who at the end of the day is going to bear the responsibility and be accountable and answerable to local church leaders and others who are organising the event.

My relationship with my workers is one of friendship, and they know that my aim is to stretch them in those areas they may need to be expanded in, yet I never dishonour them or ask them to do something I would not be willing to do myself.

The age of the worker is not important to me, and they have ranged from twelve years to those over sixty. They have found it to be indirectly as much a training programme and time of blessing for them as it has been for the children. Also, their position in their local church means little while in the Glorie Company, and again I have had principal leaders from very large fellowships and an ordained vicar. Although they will never end up being mainly children's workers, they came to learn and have their eyes opened to what God could do in children, and were able to take what they had seen back to their local flock.

I don't want to leave out any who are under twelve if what I do can be of help in training them, but I do not call these workers. Instead I call them helpers, and although they participate in nearly everything the leaders do, they don't of course bear the responsibility.

As a leader I also have a responsibility to be honest with members on my team. Having to choose so many helpers I have sometimes chosen a few wrong people whose hearts were not really for the children; they may have just wanted to get a free place at the event. With these folk—and I would stress that they are very few and far between—I share with them my concerns and sometimes even have to explain to them that unless certain attitudes change they will be little use to either children or the kingdom. I hate doing this, but as a leader this has to be done. There is a way of doing it which is not totally destructive, a way which gives that person a few positive comments, or even how things can be amended. And even after I have shared with them, I must still impress upon them that this is just my opinion, and if they feel that my analysis is incorrect about them then they have every right to ignore it, but it would be worth their while to talk the whole issue over with their local leaders when they get home.

Here, in my opinion, are some essential qualifications for a children's worker.

(1) Their walk with God has to be real and genuine

However much talent and gifting a person may have, it will not achieve much if he is not close to the Lord. He may be a genius with sports and games, music, puppets, story telling, creativity, and so the list goes on, but that person will in the long term be more of a hindrance than a help if he is not willing to get his life sorted out. Leaders have been guilty for a long time of giving talented people jobs and responsibilities just to keep them in fellowship, and at the end of the day it has only brought sadness and heartache. The old days of anyone will do to work with children is over. The children deserve the best: those who are all out for God. It must follow then that the worker must be able to know and define the voice of God unless he is regularly talking and listening to God himself.

Once he has explained biblically how we hear the voice of God, he must follow this with personal practical sharing that is earthed and comes from his own day-to-day experience. This is going to be one of the most important things a child needs to really understand; as well as leading them out of the traps of temptation, it will lead along the straight and narrow path that the Lord has set for them and save them a lot of confusion and heartache.

(2) Bible knowledge

The worker does not need to be trained at theological college, but he does need to have a good overall view of scripture, and also know how to study properly the passage of scripture that he is sharing. Prepacked children's notes, which are all ready simply to shove in the microwave and then dish out, were never meant to be the lazy way out, and although they can give some useful and helpful ideas, they really are only a foundation for you to build on. It is still vital that the worker learns how to use a cross-reference Bible, knows where and how to discover the setting and context of the passage, and tries his hardest not to add little comments that are not really there. In preparation for a talk you will probably only use a small percentage of your background research, but at least you learn a lot through your preparation, and hopefully you should have an answer for that difficult question that is sure to be asked. You will feel quite accomplished when you have an answer, and you do not have to rely on being able to waffle on until the child gets bored and wished that he had never asked the question to start with.

(3) Ability to stay in command

Amid all the noise, laughter and fun, a leader's responsibility is to see that things don't get out of hand and that the children are not allowed to become wild and unruly. A leader needs to know how to be firm and serious. Discipline is an important part of training, and children feel more secure in an environment where they know that someone is in charge. On the other hand, I do not believe that we ever have the right to smack any child, and I would be furious if any of my workers thought that they should. In my experience, I have found some school teachers in Christian work far too strict, to the point of undoing any good that has been built up.

Remember, a children's club is not school and you don't have to carry on the teacher/pupil image. It is very hard for some teachers to drop this after all their training. In cases of bad behaviour, a stern word is enough, and with the thousands of children from different backgrounds I've worked with, it has never been a major problem. Without meaning to sound super-spiritual, I guess this is because I believe that the power of the Lord is present, and also the children don't think about being naughty if they are really enjoying themselves.

(4) Your example

Whatever else you are when you are working with children you are always an example, sometimes a bad one, but hopefully usually a good one. They are going to learn more from who you are and the way you act, than they will from what you teach. I find this quite a challenge.

(5) Life and fun

Although there are pressures facing our children, they are naturally full of bounce, life and fun. I believe that the Christian has life more abundant, or lives life to the full. Well, either way you look at this, it must mean that not just children, but we too as God's children have a life that is fun and exciting. How much life and fun do children see in you as you stand out at the front of a meeting, claiming to be full of the joy of the Lord first thing on Sunday morning? I hear one person who wants to justify his miserable exterior by saying that his joy is deep down, not surface level, and the Lord knows you and loves you. Well, I'm glad to hear that. All you need to do now is ask the Lord to bring that deep joy up to the surface and then I believe you will be more of a blessing to others, and maybe they will love you as well.

It's no use you saying that you love to be with children if they don't love being with you. The classic example is when you ask the children to get into two teams, you will lead one and Johnny will lead the other. It's very embarrassing when all the children rush to be with Johnny, even your own children. Some children will want to be with exciting and fun-loving people, others will want to be with someone they feel they can trust and who won't embarrass them by being too over the top. You need to be able to portray the fruit of the Spirit in your own life in order to have the children's love and respect.

(6) Real and honest

Leading people should never be a performance. Many a church leader has failed to communicate with his congregation because every time he is in public view he looks like perfection itself, but in his mind, in his home, and in his relationships with other people, he is a completely different person, a real Dr Jeckyll and Mr Hyde personality. I believe that the day of putting on a show just to impress people is over. The average person needs to see his leaders as they really are, warts and all; a person who, like them, has to confess before God his shortcomings and the odd failure, but also a person whose heart is after God. Even in the Bible God chose to highlight the faults and sin of his greatest heroes—not so that we could think less of them; no, more that we could relate to them and learn from their faults as well as the numerous good things that they did.

When working with children we must not put ourselves on a pedestal which is higher than where we are really at; it is nothing short of a con. There may be times when we arrive at a meeting after a very busy or difficult week, or there may be a time when we may be a bit confused in our guidance. These are the times when without going into great detail, we need to ask the children to pray for us. We leaders are so often frightened of becoming vulnerable, and yet we love it when our listeners are.

Please hear me right. If you have some major ongoing problem, this must be shared with your church leaders, not the children. It would be madness to confess some sexual sin or spend your whole meeting telling the children of all your woes; the poor little things arrived so happy, but went away so depressed having had to take on board all your problems as well as their own. I think you know what I am trying to say.

Also, I would never encourage children to relate to their leaders as uncles and aunties. Apart from being untruthful and confusing, they are unbiblical terms. While still teaching respect for those older and in authority, I do believe that respect also needs to be earned. Titles can be a barrier, and I want children to relate to children's workers on a friendly yet respectful level. All my team, whatever age they are, are known by their Christian or nickname. This they have written across the fronts of their tee-shirts or jumpers so that not only can the children remember who they are, but, more to the point, so can I!

If you feel strongly that older leaders should not be called by their Christian names—after all, they may feel embarrassed if a child calls them Horace or Gertrude—may I suggest using Mr, Mrs or Miss, or whatever their title is, which of course the child is used to saying at school. This would still be much more appropriate than the meaningless words, uncle and aunty.

(7) Freedom in expressing our fun and worship

Although it may sound strange to put these two together, I suppose what I really mean is that we need

211

to be people with very few inhibitions, and not just find freedom when we are with the children and lose it when we are with adults. It's no use teaching the children an action chorus and then not doing it yourself, and it's no use trying to hide behind a guitar or piano, because with the little beady eyes of children watching there is no hiding place.

Also with praise and worship, if you are encouraging the children to express this through dance, raising their hands, kneeling, and so on, again it needs to be part of what we do naturally, not just something we teach and encourage others to participate in.

If you are bound and inhibited in your outward expression, may I suggest that you pray and ask the Lord to release you, as a lot of this may be due to your past and upbringing. For many it is quite a hard task to shake off years of inhibition and may take a little while. However, I do believe that with God's help, no matter how much of an introvert you think you are, if you really desire to be more free, God will fulfil the desire of your heart.

If it is any encouragement to you, it took me ages to be free enough to express my praise in dance. I made all the usual excuses about how stupid I would look, how I was too fat, too short, and even had what seemed like two left feet, but deep down I knew that my problem was that I was too embarrassed and too scared. I am thankful to God that he helped me through these insecurities, and I know that my work with children would have been a lot less effective had I just stayed with my feet planted firmly on the floor.

(8) Using the spiritual gifts, portraying the Spirit-filled fruit

In this book I have talked a lot about the supernatural gifts of the Holy Spirit. May I emphasise that I need to be a regular user of these gifts and not just expect the children to be. I have mentioned here the spiritual gifts rather than the spiritual fruit, not because they are more important, but because I feel little is said, written, taught and practised about the spiritual gifts with children. It should go without saying that the fruit of the Spirit mentioned in Galations 5 as 'Love, joy, peace, patience, kindness, goodness, faithfulness, gentleness and self-control', should be visibly obvious in our lives for the children to see. In all the wonderful and supernatural ways that God is using us, our growth rate in the Christian life can be calculated and discoverd not by how much the gifts are being used, but by how much the above qualities (the fruit), are being cultivated and allowed to blossom and grow.

To sum up, when talking about setting an example, the fact that we must always remember is that we cannot be leaders unless we lead.

Here are eight qualities I would want to see in those who want to work with children.

(1) They are not only willing to give to children, but they are also open to receive from them.

(2) They have a pure and innocent love for children.

(3) They believe that children are not only important in the present, but they also have a future and they in fact are the future.

(4) They believe that they are not an inferior part of the church of Christ, nor the most important people in the church; they are normal members of the body of Christ, and they need to let them know that they are.

(5) They would desire to equip the children with everything that God has made available to them, so that the children can live victoriously in a world that will often be hostile to them.

(6) They want to see the children grow in the Christian faith, and by passing on their baton to them, train them up so that in time they will be even more spiritually successful and have achieved more for the kingdom than even the teacher has.

(7) They must get the balance of never forgetting that they are working with children, and always remembering that they are working with young spiritual beings who have a large spiritual capacity that needs satisfying.

(8) They must be able to relate to other people, not just children but people of their own age group. I find it unhealthy when someone is interested only in children and has only children for friends. This is not normal.

Finally for those who are involved with organising teams, it might help you see the form that my wife, Irene, produced to send out to our would-be workers. Please forgive the overlap on what I have just said.

Glorie Company Guidelines

The vision

The Glorie Company came into being through a concept and vision that Ishmael had several years ago.

The objective

The main aims and objectives are:

(1) To lead children and young people to salvation through the Lord Jesus Christ.

(2) To encourage them to have a continual relationship with him through prayer, Bible teaching and the fullness and gifts of the Holy Spirit.

(3) To encourage them to have right attitudes and relationships with each other as Christians, by praying and ministering to each other.

(4) To show them that the Christian life is one of happiness, excitement, joy, and is not boring. To make this world a better place to live in, through the influence of our lives by example.

(5) To help them realise that though they are young, God cares, and that they are just as important to the body of Christ as anyone else.

(6) To show them they are loved and needed; they are not an unnecessary nuisance and should never be rejected, ignored, patronised, or neglected by the church.

> People were bringing little children to Jesus to have him touch them, but the disciples rebuked them. When Jesus saw this, he was indignant. He said to them, 'Let the little children come to me, and do not hinder them, for the kingdom of God belongs to such as these. I tell you the truth, anyone who will not receive the Kingdom of God like a little child will never enter it.' And he took the children in his arms, put his hands on them and blessed them (Mk 10:13–16).

The team

Ishmael's main ministry is musically orientated, therefore his band make up the nucleus of his team with Irene, his wife, as administrator/secretary. On large-scale events an excellent team of people join him, and over the years, under Ishmael's training and supervision, they have become key children's workers in their own right. Ishmael firmly believes in training others so that they can be used more effectively in their own local fellowships. Those wishing to be on the team must have a heart for children and young people, must like working with them, and ideally see a future working within that age group. Their motive for working on the team must be in that context.

Ishmael stipulates that those working in his team must be born again, Spirit-filled Christians. They should be fairly mature in their faith and based in a local church or fellowship where they have the confidence and respect of their elders, leaders or minister, who would, if asked, be willing to provide a reference to recommend them.

After people have been accepted onto the team, as well as being given all the day-to-day details of the programme, they would also be informed of the following.

Preparation

Prepare yourself spiritually so that you have lots to give to the children, and don't panic that you may not be up to it, because we will all be there to help each other.

Safety

It is vitally important that you remember that these children have been placed in our care by their parents. They are looking to us to help build up their relationship with Jesus and with their friends. This will of course include having a good time.

Safety and security is a high priority. Please do not physically handle the children. You must not pick them up, swing them around, or playfully fight with them. Accidents can easily happen, and we will be held responsible.

The children

Remember that they are on holiday and they are looking for lots of fun and friendship. Plenty of participation and movement from you as leaders will help them to relax too. Please try to be as happy, pleasant and friendly as you can. The priority is the children; we are here to serve them. Please pray for them and take special interest in their lives individually. They will come from all sorts of different backgrounds. Some will be very shy and may be frightened of being with us; others will be full of fun and mischief. Be patient and keep control.

You

We are sure that it will be a great experience for you, but children can be very demanding. Do use your free time to relax and enjoy each other's company, and try to be aware of anyone in the team who needs practical help or friendship. We are all living in close proximity, so do also respect each other's privacy.

The Glorie Company standards

Over the years Ishmael has striven to build a team of high reputation. He intends to maintain these standards and profile—to bring glory to God. We are known to have the liveliest children's workers around, and he expects one hundred per cent energy and commitment one hundred per cent of the time. You will be expected to give hours of bouncing, shouting and ministering during the week.

Ishmael also expects his team to be mature enough to comply with the following three rules:

* No gossip or criticising of each other.
* No barbed humour. There will be no pulling down, getting at each other or disrespect using cruel jokes or bad humour.

* No crude or sick jokes.

These things are not 'fun' and are not in keeping with our image, nor do they glorify the Lord Jesus whom we serve. we should respect, honour and encourage each other at all times.

In hard print this may sound very strict, but clearly defining the rules is important when forming a team of people.

I realise that halfway through the week some will be physically and spiritually exhausted, and some of the worst parts of their characters are likely to start showing. We are prepared for this and many times have been able to pray into workers' lives and see them return home at the end of the week having been transformed in one area or another by the power of God.

Adrian Plass has reminded me that an anagram of Ishmael is 'I lash 'em'. As a leader, my team members may say 'Amen' to that! But I'm sure they realise that underneath this confident, harsh exterior beats the heart of a man who, in working with children, is still very much in the learning process.

Every book has to end somewhere, and although there is still so much more I could say, I'm running out of time and pages.

Let me conclude by saying that we are experiencing a unique generation of children. The main reason that some people may find some of the things I have written about hard to swallow is because many of the things I have mentioned didn't happen to them when they were children.

I believe there are two reasons why this new generation of young people is so hungry for God. The first is that they are being prepared for persecution, but they will not fear it. Far from it, they will thrive and grow from strength to strength because of it.

I am reminded of a Baptist church which was holding a family service, and the children were on the platform doing a dramatic production in front of their parents and the rest of the congregation. Afterwards, the minister felt that the Lord wanted to speak through him to all present. As he started speaking he didn't have a clue what he was going to say, and if he had, I doubt very much if he would have had the courage to say it. He made statements about the children that they had been watching; some would be persecuted for their faith, and some would even be martyred. This, understandably, was too much for the parents and close friends to cope with and many broke down in tears.

It was at this point that all eyes were directed to the platform and the children. They saw an amazing sight. Far from being scared by what they had heard, the children had spontaneously fallen on their knees and were rejoicing and praising God with their hands raised.

God is building up and equipping a little army where warfare is going to be the norm, and every soldier on the battlefield will learn to cope with pressures and dangerous times.

Secondly, they are being prepared for a mighty outpouring of God's Holy Spirit on the unsaved. Call it revival if you like, but unlike similar happenings of old, they will not only be equipped to see people saved and filled with the power of God, but they will also have warm, friendly and untraditional fellowships to bring them to. Those who have been completely outside of the faith will be nurtured without being lost.

I could be wrong, but I could be right! I plead with you to start giving children the very best of everything that God has for them while they are still young.

The History of Ishmael

by Ian Smale

Ishmael—what do you make of him?

Don't think of an answer just now—suspend judgement for a while, and let him speak for himself.

Tongues before the 'charismatic movement'. Early rock 'n' roll at the Girl Guides. Life on the farm (it shouldn't happen to a choirboy). And the price of fame, the serious truth behind the humorous stage image.

It's all here, told as only Ishmael could tell it.

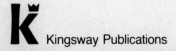

Kingsway Publications